Remember

A Little Book of Courage, Comfort and Hope

Joy —
   I've been a big
fan of yours for years —
Please —— Just make
more movies!

   Wishing you Peace!
Joy in the new year!

♡

Paula Boynton

Other Books by Paul Boynton

Books available at beginwithyes.com

- Begin with Yes
- Begin with Yes - 10th Anniversary Edition
- Be Amazing
- Begin with Yes Nighttime Affirmations
- Begin with Yes 21 Day Companion Workbook
- Begin with Yes – Action Planner
- Commit - Transform Your Body and Your Life with the Power of Yes
- Beginnings - A Daily Guide for Adventurous Souls
- Begin with Yes: At Work for You

Also available:

- Begin with Yes 21 Day Workbook Online Course

What People Are Saying

"Paul Boynton is the good angel on your shoulder, reminding you to just listen to your heart. What a gift Paul has for putting reassurance into straightforward and easily digestible language, and what a gift this book is for anybody who could use it (the whole world)."

– Ernest Thompson – Academy Award-winning author of *On Golden Pond*

"A little light on cloudy days can make all the difference. This little book is that light."

– Mark Dagostino - *Seven-time NY Times Bestselling Co-Author of books that uplift and inspire*

"This little book is exactly what the world needs right now. It's filled with love and grounded-in-reality optimism that will shift your thinking, lift your spirits, and help you move through the challenging times we all experience… and welcome more joy, too!"

– SARK – author, *Succulent Wild Woman*, PlanetSARK.com

"I pick this book up often to help me remember that I am resilient, and that every storm passes. And I share it with my friends whenever they could use a little encouragement and hope, too."

– Tshidi Mayne, Broadway's *The Lion King*

"There was this spark that happened when you were born. It represented an event that had never happened before and will never happen again so long as the universe endures. That spark is you. It's powerful, creative, curious, resourceful ... capable of creating a life that matters. Paul Boynton has spent his writing career reminding us of the hope, courage, and joy that we all have in our true natures. This new book, *Remember*, comes along at the perfect time to remind us humans that we matter, that we belong here, and that we can create a world that is loving, equal, and has so much more than enough for all of us to live together well. Thank you for helping us remember, Paul."

– Jacob Nordby, author *The Creative Cure: How Finding and Freeing Your Inner Artist Can Heal Your Life*

When to Seek Professional Help

We were not created to be perfect; we were created to be real. Real people make mistakes, take wrong turns, and disappoint themselves and others even when they're doing the best they can.

Some paths we find ourselves walking can be overwhelming and shake us to our very core. There is nothing we or anyone else can do to make it go away, and we may feel powerless, frightened, and alone.

The hopeful, positive messages in this book will help you remember that every storm passes. At the same time, we know that some storms are more powerful than others and we are not always expected or able to manage these major storms all by ourselves.

I was trained as a counselor and social worker and have personally benefitted from individual and couple's therapy. I know from my own experience that we were created to grow and learn and evolve, and sometimes we may need additional professional help to make that happen. If you feel you need some extra guidance or assistance moving forward, I fully support and encourage you to continue that journey.

Introduction

You and I may not know each other personally, and we may never get a chance to meet face-to-face to share a cup of coffee, but I know you.

I know you are a good person. You are kind and thoughtful and you want things to go better, feel better, and be better, too. And I know you want all that not just for yourself, but for all the other people who grace your life. Our stories might be a bit different, and we may have taken different trains with different stops and delays along the way, but you and I have always been on the same tracks. And that's why you feel, or soon will feel, like you know me, too.

I know what it's like to feel happy, safe, focused, secure, productive and grounded. And I know how it feels to be lonely, scared, confused, anxious, scattered, and uncertain. I know what it's like to be shaken to the core, stuck, sad and worried. I have had easy times and harder times, good days and not-so-good days. I have had successes and victories, and I've made mistakes, and taken wrong turns, too.

You see, you and I have a lot in common. And although we may live different lives and have different realities to deal with, we share so much when it comes to living imperfect lives.

Now that you've been reminded of my *realness*, you may be thinking this doesn't sound like a person who should be writing self-help books like this one, or my others, *Begin with Yes* and *Be Amazing*. But if you're one of the over two million friends on my social media pages named after these two books, you probably won't be totally caught off guard, and you'll know why I am the perfect person to be writing these books. It's because I believe in the life-changing power of *optimism grounded in reality*. I visualize this concept as one foot in midair, making my personal dreams come true, while keeping one foot on the ground, dealing with all the realities that are mine and mine, alone.

So often when I interact with my online or *virtual family*, I am continually humbled and grateful to read the almost-daily comments people leave after reading my inspirational posts. Things like, "How did you know I needed to hear this, today?" Or "This could not come at a more perfect time for me." I always smile when I read these notes because I realize that what people are really saying is, "I am a real person too, just like you." And because of that, when I write from my heart, our hearts connect, real-person to real-person. We are all in-sync in some amazing and beautiful ways, and that very fact makes me (and I hope you, too) feel less alone in the world.

I believe that we are not created to be perfect; we are created to be *real*. And real people living real lives need to feel less lonely and less alone. During the good times, we share courage comfort and hope with others. Yet during more challenging times, we could all use a little courage comfort and hope headed our way, too.

I hope this little book can be that for you.

Louis Armstrong had it right when he sang, "What a wonderful world." But truth be told, Louis Armstrong also faced a lifetime of challenges that would seemingly prove this song wrong, time and time again. If you and I really do somehow know each other, it's partly because we have seen and experienced the beautiful parts of life. And we have also been challenged and discouraged by some of the more difficult, disappointing, painful, and heartbreaking aspects of living a real life, too

Like Mr. Armstrong, we might wish for a 'wonderful world,' but deep down we know it's a bit more complicated than that. Slowly, we begin to realize that wonderful is not really a time or place, instead it's a choice we make over and over. There isn't a train that will take us to a town called "Wonderful," rather it's a trip that takes place in our hearts, and in our minds. It's not a final stop or ultimate destination, but rather a comfortable state of mind that we need to remember and visit as often as we can.

Remembering sounds easy, and here's why it isn't as easy as we'd like to think: we often must work through a few complications and challenges to find our way back home. And it's not usually a one-time trip, but an adventure we need to take over and over again.

When many of us look to social media for connection or support, or even guidance, it would seem pretty evident that life sure seems to be wonderful for just about everyone else, except us. At the same time, if we consulted news broadcasts and newspapers, we might assume the world is falling apart and sadly beyond repair. So understandably, when we survey what's around us to get a sense of reality, it can be confusing to find this dichotomy. Our assumption is that the world is mostly more wonderful for other people, and at the same time, it's basically in tatters and spinning out of control for the rest of us. And even more disappointing, deep down we may begin to suspect, that a "wonderful world" is just a nice song, and not an accurate picture of our lives.

But there is reason for hope.

There is one place we don't often look for our answers, and that's *inside*. When we look within, we begin to pay attention to how we are feeling in the moment. And that's when, especially if we are feeling discouraged, we can choose to remember or be reminded of other things that almost always help us feel a little bit, or very often quite a bit, better.

This little book you are holding in your hand right now, and I hope in your heart, too, was written to help you rediscover - or remember - the pathways that are inside of you. In fact, I suspect this book has found you at the absolute perfect time and you are more than ready for what you will begin to remember. I bet, like me, you are profoundly tired of the 24-hour news cycle, and I'd also bet you're tired of hearing about everyone else's perfect family, perfect job, perfect vacations and if not perfect, pretty-darn-close-to-perfect lives.

To begin with, let's remember that the world isn't wonderful because it's perfect. It's wonderful, *despite* its imperfections.

You should also know that most of my writing isn't that of a teacher, but rather from the perspective of a guide. It's a journal of my ups and downs, and good days and bad days, that I simply share with you.

In other words, I write from my heart and often what I write about are things I need to remember. And thus, the title of this new book: *Remember – A Little Book of Courage, Comfort and Hope* was born.

I've shared some of my favorite inspirational quotes from my social media pages, newly edited and expanded, and I've also added some new material that will eventually find their way to those pages. And finally, I have made a few personal notes scattered throughout to add depth and context, and to share more of my journey with you.

When times are tough, these thoughts will help you remember and will help calm the storm. They will help you feel less alone, and they'll remind you that every storm passes, and when you least expect it, the stars will once again begin to peer out from the nighttime sky. And they will help you realize that despite the challenges, Louis Armstrong was actually right all along.

It *is* a wonderful world.

Now, I have a confession to make. I have been struggling to write this message to you for a while, now. When I traveled to New York City not long ago, I suddenly discovered I had a few days to myself. It was then my heart finally found its voice.

I was staying in a hotel and the housekeeper tending to my room was a very kind, older woman from Cambodia. Her name was Sopheap, and she had been working in the city as a hotel housekeeper for over 42 years. We saw each other briefly each morning and slowly, to our delight and surprise, discovered a comradery and unexpected kinship. I knew when it was time for me to pack up and go home, it was likely we would never meet again, but something inside me suspected that our meeting - though fleeting - would be life-altering.

Sopheap's English was somewhat limited, and, let's face it, my Cambodian was non-existent, so we did our level best to communicate in the simplest ways we could. She told me about coming to this country, the house that she lived in (which was a long subway ride from the hotel), her sore neck, and the familiar chore of making dinner each night. Then she stopped for a moment and talked about her pride in saving money so her elderly mother could return to Cambodia to visit once again. All of a sudden, I saw her eyes glisten as she was moved to tears while she continued to touch upon a memory I couldn't fully understand but was deeply meaningful to her. Slightly embarrassed, I saw she quickly wiped her eyes with the tail of her shirt. It was then I realized my eyes had welled, too.

As she told me all these 'jewels' of her life, I watched as she casually continued to fluff the pillows of my bed and instinctively continue on with the duties of her day. I saw her install fresh bedding and then carefully "iron" the sheets with her hands, fluidly smoothing out the wrinkles. All of these effortless details she did with precision, elegance and grace, and with a smile never far from her face.

The talk then turned to the bottles of my medicine she spotted on the counter, and her playfully teasing me that I requested more towels. An easy, lighthearted banter found us.

Two strangers a world apart, who delighted in every somewhat-fragmented story they shared.

On one of my last days seeing her in the hotel, I watched as she rummaged through her purse and presented me with a small bottle. I learned it was some type of medicine from Cambodia. She pointed to her nose and rubbed it, to show it was good for a cold. Then she touched her temples, suggesting it would help a headache. Finally, she rubbed her stomach and I managed to understand that adding a few drops of this potion to hot water would expertly soothe a belly ache.

Although many of the spoken words we both tried to share with one another seemed to fall through the cracks, we did understand almost everything in the language of heart-to-heart, tear-to-tear, and laugh-to-laugh. We connected in each of those moments, and it was wonderful.

I have, over time, grown to believe that we can find that 'wonderful world' in the most unlikely of places. It's in the simple connection we can find with others when we least expect it. Even while living in a world filled with uncertainty, it's our realness that makes the beautiful world, possible.

And so, I dedicate this book to all of you. Those who have reached out to me, and those who I hope to hear from one day soon. This book is for each one of you.

And it's for Sopheap. I will always remember the tears and the laughter we shared. They are, and were, and forever will be, sacred. You make this world beautiful. And I promise, I will always remember you.

Now it's our turn. Let's remember, together.

Every Storm Passes

If you're going through a difficult, painful, lonely time, be assured that this is a natural part of the human experience. And even though we know every fire burns out and every storm passes, this moment in time can often leave you feeling shaken and confused, frightened and sad. Keep breathing, rest, and shift your attention - even for a moment or two - to more hopeful thoughts. You are more resilient than you may be feeling, and I promise, the dark clouds will one day pass.

This one speaks to me as much as it may be speaking to you. These really difficult times are not speed bumps or minor detours, they are 'gut punches' that can leave us feeling confused and even floundering. I have been in this just-keep-breathing place many times, and if the 'breathing' part seems like all you can manage in this very moment, that is enough. You will regain your footing soon. Inhale. Exhale. Repeat.

When You Feel, You Heal

Cleaning out a basement or attic or even a closet can frequently spark a walk down memory lane. And these memories can often be mixed. Even the happy ones can sometimes evoke feelings that are sad or overwhelming. The walk can be difficult, and physically and emotionally draining, too, but it's a clear sign you're ready to look forward, not backward. As the heart opens a bit, the arms do, too - a clear sign that you are now ready to embrace the good that is yet to come.

It's so easy putting off those major clearing-out projects because it's a daunting task. The more we postpone the inevitable, however, the more the clutter continues to pile up. When I have done those major purges, it has always been a cathartic experience, and the exhilarating feeling afterward, borders on joy. You begin with the junk drawer and see how that goes.

(A big thank you to my good friend, Susan Bastien, for allowing me to use her insightful saying, "When you feel, you heal." She's an amazing massage therapist, whose hands feel what her clients are going through and allow her to offer them healing, comfort and encouragement.)

Be Patient With Yourself

There are cycles in our lives with good days, weeks and even months, but there are also cycles with difficult and challenging times. There is no easy solution for those difficult times. But it may help to remember that we all experience these ebbs and flows. Remind yourself that the getting-through part will eventually pass, and that moving even the smallest of small steps forward can, and will, make a difference.

I think that's why I have always been drawn to solitary walks along the ocean. The consistency and reliability of shifting tides reminds me on some deeper level that things will eventually feel more manageable and often, better. Try stepping outdoors where you can reconnect with the world around you to see if that provides a bit of "in your soul" relief.

You Deserve to be Happy!

For now, act as if you deserve to be happy and fulfilled. Eventually your mind will catch up with your heart.

This is where that 'fake it 'til you make it' bit of advice comes in handy. Because I've written so many books on positivity, people often expect that I will always be optimistic and positive. So often I have to act confident, brave, or even happy, when I am not really feeling any of those things. When I do put on this 'face', I've learned that the feeling eventually catches up to me. And in some situations, I'll admit that I have to take a deep breath, smile and simply take a step forward. Usually acting positive soon becomes 'feeling' positive. At the same time, I have struggles and disappointments and major stormy days - even weeks. I don't feel like I have to smile my way through major upsets, and you don't need to, either. Practice acting happy when you can, and this will help you find easier days more often than not. And remember this: you do deserve to be happy. Honest-to-God.

Let Go and Feel Lighter

If it feels like you have the weight of the world on your shoulders, it's time to let go of some serious baggage. For starters, let go of responsibilities that belong to others. Let go of things beyond your control. Let go of past mistakes and regrets. Let go. Let go. Let go. Lighter. Lighter. Lighter.

It helps me to actually name, and say out loud, what I am going to let go of. And I also need to remember that it's not always a permanent letting go. Sometimes, it's just taking a break from letting go. Both help.

Small Steps Create Opportunities

So often we wait for the universe to show up and help us make things happen, forgetting that it actually works the other way around. When we show up and take even the smallest of steps, the universe and the powers-that-be join in to help keep things moving in the right direction. No matter where you are or how you're feeling, you can take one small step forward, today.

I keep a list of multiple big goals with me and try to take at least one small step towards two or three of them, every day. Remember the small steps are often easy to do; they may take less than fifteen minutes, sometimes even less than two minutes and they create a rhythm to your day that will give you a sense of true progress. And many times, when I take a small step, suddenly an opportunity to take a couple more appears and before I even realize it, I continue to move forward, and my progress continues.

Create Healthy Boundaries

We need to learn the difference between having a willingness to be kind, open and forgiving, and being a doormat. One allows us to maintain our dignity and self-respect, and the other leaves us with a pit in the stomach. Once you know the difference, your behavior will change, forever.

Trust your intuition. It's almost always right.

A Small Difference is Still a Difference

I do not know the answer to all the violence, evil and darkness in the world, but I do know the response. It is your warm, unexpected smile as you pass a stranger on the street. It is speaking up and standing up for those who are being discriminated against. It's letting others know that we are much more alike, than we are different.

I sometimes feel overwhelmed by the magnitude and depth of suffering in the world. If I watch the news on TV, I almost always feel moments of despair, too. Then, I remind myself that I am also surrounded by little things that are easy to do that can make a difference in someone else's life. I have never been disappointed with the results of a sincere, unexpected warm smile shared with a stranger, either.

Tonight, Rest Easy

When our heads finally hit the pillow tonight, let's think about the smiles of the people we love – those nearby, those far away, and those who make up the sweet and beautiful memories that will stay with us forever. Remembering each smile is a way to count your blessings and invites sleep to gently find you. Let go of any thoughts that will keep you from resting peacefully. You can always reclaim them tomorrow, in the light of day.

When you are feeling fearful, tense, depressed, worried or stuck, just remember you are a survivor. You are so much stronger and so much more capable than you may feel in this one moment. If you don't believe me, just look at all you've already dealt with and remind yourself – you're still here! So tonight, rest easy.

Your Dreams Count

Just for today, act as if your dreams count. Just for today, believe you deserve people in your life who are respectful, honest, and make you feel good about yourself. Just for today, don't listen to anyone who holds you back, keeps you stuck or makes you unhappy. Just for today, take a small and deliberate step towards your dreams. And then tomorrow, there's a very good chance you'll want another day like today.

Often this requires a bit of being your own cheerleader. It helps to write a note to carry in your pocket, or a text you send to yourself that that says, "My dreams count, too, and making them happen is up to me."

Moving Through Fear

It's not so much about eliminating fear, it's much more about taking those small steps, despite the fear. Walking forward through the fear is the goal, and you can do it.

Feeling fear is such a routine part of my life. But if I let fear stop me, I wouldn't get anything done! That being said, I'll admit it has slowed me down more times than I can count. I am working on this, too. And I've also noticed that when I do move through the fear, to my great surprise, the fear itself dissipates rather quickly.

Patience Takes Practice

A life-changing breakthrough is like a flower that suddenly bursts into bloom. It usually happens after we send for the seed catalog, place the order, prepare the soil, fertilize the ground, read the directions, plant the seed, water daily, and then patiently wait with a mixture of determination, hope and faith.

Sometimes the breakthroughs in my life have happened at unexpected times. We don't always control the timeline. Sometimes we have to practice patience and other times, we get those results even faster than expected. I like the faster one's better, but a breakthrough anytime is welcomed and the result of many small steps that have finally added up.

Not Your Job

Obviously, we are called to love, help and encourage other people. But one very common mistake is trying to make someone else (or everyone else) happy. It just can't be done. Instead, we need to turn our attention and our energy towards our own goals and dreams – things that we feel passion for. By doing that, we actually show others how to seek happiness for themselves.

For people like me, this is easy to understand and especially difficult to put in practice. I want everyone to be happy and I spend way too much time and energy trying to keep everyone around me happy. This is a reminder that I need to read over and over and over. So, I remember and then turn my attention to my own work and goals. And then I forget and have to be reminded, again. I have actually encouraged those closest to me to remind me whenever they like. It helps.

Trust Your Inner Voice

Being afraid of our inner voice that tells us something we don't really want to hear is human. Listening anyway, is courageous.

I once saw a bumper sticker that read, "What do you know that you're not letting yourself see?" As it turns out, quite a bit. Remember, not seeing doesn't change what's real; it just allows you to temporarily stay in limbo and remain uncomfortable and stuck. So, try a bit harder to listen. Then rest, if you need to. And then, listen some more.

Slow Change is Still Change

One-step-at-a-time can sometimes be measured in minutes. One less minute spent worrying today is a goal every single one of us could achieve. And if we replace that minute of worry with a minute of peaceful and loving thoughts, those minutes will slowly add up and our minds will begin to shift in wonderful ways.

Now would be a good time to remind you that I share this strategy from a place of needing to do this, too. I am not naive or out of touch with how hard it can be to worry less. I am absolutely doing this right along with you, one minute at a time. Hopefully, you aren't disappointed with this admission. In fact, hopefully, you'll just feel like you are in good company!

Be Authentic

Other people may try to manage you by suggesting you should meet their expectations about who you should be. It's simply not true. The best way to be a loving and kind person is to stay focused on what you're about, what you want to happen, and what's important to you. It's not selfish; it's authentic. And isn't that what we want to share with our partners, lovers, and friends?

It's always struck me as ironic and somewhat sad that the people who want to know us and love us, also want to manage us. They want us to be authentic, but that seems to happen in ways that jive with the picture they have in their head about who we are. You can't have it both ways. But that doesn't mean that the people we love most won't give it a try.

Choose Love

When you choose love even when you're struggling, you are choosing power and hope. And power and hope will hold you steady through the difficult days and gently lift you into calmer waters, soon.

Choosing love can be as simple as listening to someone else, giving someone a hug or offering a gentle smile to a child, or even a pet. Love doesn't need to be dramatic; it just needs to be real.

You are Worthy

You're beautiful and worthy of respect and hope, even if you don't agree.

It's taken me a long time to learn that how I am feeling is a 'feeling' not a 'fact.' And while I believe with all my heart that honoring our feelings is important, I also know that if we only pay attention to a feeling, we will likely get stuck. As a form of practice, when you are talking with friends, accept and honor their feelings and then gently offer them a glimpse of facts.

For example, you can say, "I understand why you are feeling scared about the job interview tomorrow. At the same time, I know you are a talented and hardworking person, and when you relax, you are so much fun to talk with." It's a way of being respectful of how someone is feeling while showing them another way to get ready for that interview. And then if you can do that for a friend, practice doing it for yourself, too.

Resilient People Make Good Friends

Most of the interesting, compassionate and influential people in the world have faced major disappointments, had their hearts broken once or twice, heard and marched to that different drum, and experienced loneliness, despair and failure. Not surprisingly, these are the same people creating beautiful art, music, dance and theatre and who have become deeply intuitive, generous and unconditional lovers.

The people I want in my life are the people who have fought some battles, fallen down a time or two, experienced hardships and failures, and kept on moving. They seem real and deeper to me, and I have learned that they are more reliable, too. The fact that they have survived and continued to grow, create, and thrive just makes them the kind of people I am most drawn to.

Your Middle Name Is Courage

Most of us are on a first-name basis with fear, but fortunately our middle name just happens to be 'courage.' So, when we meet fear on the path, we nod in recognition, but we don't engage. Instead, we hold our head high, eyes focused on the path ahead, and we keep moving towards our dreams, one small step at a time.

Fear is like a sponge; it absorbs all the power you're willing to give it. See Fear. Feel it. And then ask what it's teaching you. Then evaluate if it's worthy of the power you've bestowed on it. Most of the time, it's not.

You Are Enough

Having deep and intimate relationships can add new meaning and beauty to our lives and it is wonderful to love and be loved, cherish and be cherished. But always remember that you, all by yourself, are enough. You are complete, beautiful and whole. And with that as your starting place, you move forward not waiting for but fully expecting that you will draw other healthy, happy, complete people into your lives to share parts of the journey.

I have discovered as I grow and learn and evolve, I attract, without even trying, deeper, more interesting, and healthier people into my world. Do your homework, keep learning, push yourself just a little bit further or deeper, and people who deserve you will find you.

Big Dreams and Small Steps

Don't talk yourself out of those big goals or dreams. We need more people to think big and I believe you know in your heart and soul that you have important things to accomplish, important things to share and important goals to accomplish. Say YES to what could be and then just BEGIN by taking a small step. Believing in yourself is not arrogant, or self-absorbed, or wrong. In fact, it's just the opposite. The world needs you to live up to your potential and there's no time like right now to take that next step.

I didn't write and publish my first book because I thought I was a great writer. I grew and began believing in myself as an author, because I actually wrote that first book. For me, my ability to believe in myself deepened when I actually dared to embrace my big ideas and goals. In other words, I wasn't able to embrace big dreams and goals because I believed in myself, I went after the goals and dreams and with each small step, my self-esteem and self-respect took those steps forward with me.

New Questions, New Opportunities

You will never have all the answers because each answer creates new questions. There's a sweet rhythm when you remember that one question, one answer, one-step-at-a-time is how life is meant to unfold. It's kind of like breathing, while you're asleep.

Sometimes I find that I think so hard with my head that I don't hear what my heart is shouting. I am also learning I don't and can't figure out the next ten steps – it's easier and better to think about the next one or two steps, take those and then reassess. If I try and map it all out, I can get overwhelmed, and stuck.

Follow the Yellow Brick Road

Trust that your path will unfold as you step into it. The challenge with big dreams or big problems is that they're complex, impossible to map out, and very often overwhelming to contemplate. The solution to all these roadblocks is one small step today, another one tomorrow, and then another after that.

This reminds me of the 'yellow brick road' and the one-step, or skip-at-a-time. And as far as I can tell, that worked out fairly well for everyone on that path. Taking a nonstop flight might be faster but the 'yellow brick road' proved much more fruitful.

When Love Isn't Working

The love of family, friends and romantic partners are wonderful miracles in our lives. But we can't force someone to love us. And trying to do so is a heartbreaking and terrible waste of time, energy, and self-respect. We may love someone who doesn't love us back, or who doesn't love us the way we want. We may wish to be loved by someone who can only love us on their terms and only when we appear to be who they wish we were. We must let that be and move on. We may think we need a specific person to love us a certain way, but who and how others love is not up to us to decide. We must let that be and move on.

Having had the experience of loving someone who wasn't really available in the same way or at the same time to love me back, I know how difficult moving on can be. I actually needed professional help with this and even then, moving on was a struggle.

What finally worked for me took the support of friends, a skilled therapist who spoke her mind, and then some time. It's not easy. You may take a step forward and then two steps backwards. Persevere. And there will be a turning point. Moving on doesn't often happen without pain or tears or missteps but you can, and you will, get there. And when you do, you may wonder, "What took me so long?"

Knowing When to Move On

Moving on may be sad and difficult, but it will free us to pour our energy into being, honoring and celebrating the person we truly are. And when we stop trying to be loved by specific people in specific ways, true love in all sorts of wonderful forms will surprise us again and again. Only then will we realize that those are the miracles we have been looking for, all along.

Knowing when to 'throw in the towel' and move on has always been one of the most difficult things for me. I think my optimistic nature sometimes makes me feel hopeful beyond the point of reason. In those situations, I've never been able to find the energy or conviction to move on without some help. Sometimes I am able to see things more clearly with the help of a friend, but other times, it's been much more difficult. All this to say, if you don't know how or when to move on, it's never a bad time to ask for help.

Close Your Eyes and Open Your Heart

Be afraid, but don't be stopped. Be confused, but don't be stuck. Be worn out, but don't give up. You've done it before, and you can do it again. And then, when you get under the covers tonight put it all aside, close your eyes and open your heart so the universe can restore and heal, and get you ready for another day!

When I love, appreciate and accept myself, I find it easy to do it for others. And that turns into a win-win all around. It is time to love, appreciate and accept yourself as you are, and where you are, right at this very moment. And then, it is time to love, appreciate and accept yourself for where you are headed. You are worthy and lovable from this moment on.

Resilience is Your Superpower

Show me someone who hasn't fallen flat on their face a few times, and I will show you someone who is probably standing still, afraid, lonely and wishing they could be more like you. So don't let a setback hold you back. Let's see what we can make happen, today.

When I reflect on my life so far, I can spot all the setbacks I have lived through. Things like the jobs I didn't get, the publishers who weren't interested in my books, the relationships that didn't go the way I wanted, financial challenges, low credit scores, cars that wouldn't start on cold New England mornings, and the list goes on and on. But with each setback, I learned and grew.

Ironically, now I realize that what I once thought was a setback, was just a detour or course-correction that got me to better places, in unexpected ways. And the icing on the cake? Setbacks make us more resilient. And resilience is a superpower that comes from falling down and then getting back up.

Your Purpose Matters

If you've been drifting without a clear picture of your purpose, it's time to become more intentional. Begin by rediscovering your passions – often the things you were drawn to as children – or things you'd be doing if the stresses of life hadn't gotten in the way. Then, find very small steps that enliven these thoughts or dreams. If you always wanted to be a writer, get a notebook and begin writing. If you wanted to be a veterinarian, offer to volunteer at an animal shelter. As you begin taking those small steps, a purpose will gradually be revealed, and the path will appear. And that's how dreams come true.

We all drift or wander from time to time. And there have been times in my life when I've drifted way too long. Recognizing that you are drifting is Step One. Asking yourself 'why' is Step Two. Looking at your answers directly and honestly and then taking small steps to self-correct comes next. For example, if we're drifting, we need to ask ourselves, "How can I figure out what to do?" Talking to yourself in a journal may help. And once you have some ideas, following through will make all the difference.

The Mystery of Loss and Grief

When we experience a loss that leaves us brokenhearted, lonely and inconsolable, it's because the love and joy was, and is, just as powerful as our grief. And it's never really about pushing the sadness away, but about remembering and letting the joy in, too. It's in those stunningly beautiful moments that we catch a glimpse beyond the mystery and know in our hearts that love is not only stronger, it's forever.

To those missing loved ones today, maybe the loss is recent, and your grief runs deep, or maybe it's been a very long time and what's left is a lingering sense of melancholy. But either way, there's an empty space in your heart that can't quite be filled, no matter how long it's been, or how many other wonderful people are in your life to love and who are loving you back. I am not an expert on grief, although, like most of us, I have had my own experiences.

The pathway forward is different for each of us. It helps to think about what you need and ask for it. Sometimes, it's just quiet company with someone who loves and understands. Other times it's a distraction so I can rest my broken heart for a few minutes. Dealing with grief is a journey for sure, but maybe it's not something to get through, but rather something we must integrate into our lives, so the love and memories slowly become stronger than the painful feelings of loss. As you remember someone special today, may you feel their eternal presence in your heart, forever.

Be More Human

The things that have hurt you, broken your heart, made you cry with pain, grief and even rage are the very same things that have made you more human, more compassionate, and more able to help lift others into the light of unconditional love. And that's the one thing we all desperately need, and the most significant, life-changing gift we can offer.

I am so sorry if you are hurting right now. I can promise you I have been there a few times and I truly know how you feel. I can't tell you how or when you will feel better, but I can promise you that you will feel and get better. It helps to be honest with yourself. It helps to feel the pain and share it with close friends or a therapist. It helps to cry. It helps to laugh. It helps to focus on other things. And it helps to remember that you have been here before, and you have survived. The sun may not come out tomorrow, but if it's hidden by clouds for the moment, it will return soon.

When Clouds Hide the Light

The light within you may dim or flicker, but it never, ever burns out. Never.

This one is going to take a little trust on your part. I know (because I have been there) that there will be days and moments and life events that will convince you that the light is no longer there. We need people in our lives who will gently remind us that the light is not gone for good, and in turn, we need to also do that for the people in our lives. Timing is everything and sometimes we don't want to hear the sun will come out tomorrow; we just want someone to quietly sit with us. And that's okay, too.

A Burnt Potato or a Catastrophe?

Once we understand the difference between a burnt potato and a catastrophe, we will learn to smile at small upsets and live more graceful, grateful lives.

In our lives, we will have a few catastrophic moments and we will have lots of burnt potato moments. Learning how to spot the difference is easier than you might think. When you face a difficult moment, simply ask yourself, "Which one is this?"

Finding Optimism

Just because we have a hopeful and optimistic spirit doesn't mean we don't have challenging days, personal struggles and heartbreaking experiences. What it does mean is that we know it's important to surround ourselves with positive people and energy. And that we have great respect for our own resiliency and take personal responsibility for making things better.

I am often asked for advice on how to welcome more positive people into our lives. I think it starts with a clear intention. Recognizing that you do desire to have more optimistic, hopeful people in your circle is a great place to start.

It also helps to be aware of what kind of people already surround you and then choosing, in very deliberative ways, to spend more time with those who are aligned with positivity and hope. And it's not just positive people, it's the music we listen to, the television shows we watch, and the memes we share on social media. All of it can influence how we feel. Also pay attention to those times when you are feeling more hopeful and positive. This will greatly inform you and help to attract others who share your spirit and outlook.

Listen, Feel, See

What do you know that you're not letting yourself see? If you're willing to open your eyes and your heart, you just might have a breakthrough so significant, so powerful, and so wonderful that your life will never be the same. It's worth thinking about closely.

I have learned the hard way that our problem isn't always not-knowing; our problem is often not being willing to listen. And the reason we don't want to listen is we aren't ready to accept the truth. I stayed in an unhealthy relationship for a long time because I wasn't willing or able to listen to what my heart always knew. My heart felt like it was literally breaking while I ignored the reality that the relationship had run its course.

Over time, I have challenged myself to listen sooner and with less resistance and I've gotten better at it. Not perfect, but better. And over the years as I have talked to and coached other people, I have discovered that this unwillingness to listen is everywhere. So, I ask again, what do YOU know that you're not letting yourself see? And the follow up question is, "Now that you know, what might you do about it?"

Honoring Our Passions

We each have the potential to love and change the world in ways well beyond anything we could ever imagine. But the simple truth is, this won't happen unless we honor our passions and embrace the unique and beautiful person we are. So, begin there and then help others honor and embrace their own passions, too. Not only will your world change, but the world will change, too.

If you journal or want to try, spend some time writing about what makes you beautiful. For most of us, it's easier to focus on our flaws, disappointments and challenges. Spending some time writing about your amazingness should uncover a few things you may have misplaced.

A Game Changing Moment

Sometimes the smallest of actions, in retrospect, become one of the most pivotal and significant life-changing moments. That truth alone makes taking a small step today easier and worth the effort.

The funny thing about this is the 'retrospect' part. We almost never know when one of those small steps will be the game-changer. So, onward we go.

Staying the Course

Sometimes doing our best means we simply got out of bed. It means that despite the realities and challenges in our path, we still managed to put one foot in front of the other and move in the direction that makes the most sense, for now. And it means whether today was an easy or difficult day, remember to be gentle, forgiving and loving with ourselves and also with those around us who are doing their best, too.

It is sometimes easier to help others see that what looks like a small step is actual a major, positive, life-affirming step. Everything is relative and practice being as kind and as gentle with yourself as you are with others. Accept today as it was, and yourself as you were.

Letting Go Is OK

Sometimes there are people in our lives who seem to have pressed the 'self-destruct' button. They make one bad decision after another and seem to create chaos and heartbreak all around. We really do love them, but we really cannot help them and that's a frustrating and sad place to be. And so, we begin to emotionally – and often even physically – love them from a distance. We let go, so that we can share our light and love with those who are able to receive it. And we let go so that the love and light that surrounds us can be received.

This realization can be heartbreaking. Letting go can feel like an abandonment. Remember that letting go is not an act as much as a realization that you never actually were holding something, or someone, in the first place. Loving someone from afar is sometimes the very best that we can do, both for the other person and for ourselves, too.

Breathe It Out and Breathe It In

Practice letting your worries out with a sigh, and then breathing in faith, hope and self-confidence.

When I do this, I actually say to myself, "Worries out... faith or hope or self-confidence in," as I slowly breathe in and out.

You are not your worries, your fears, your anxieties or your disappointments. You are the tender touch, helping hand and gentle smile. You are here to stand up and speak out demanding fairness, opportunity and hope. You are here on purpose, and with purpose. You have everything you need, and the world is waiting. When you're gentle with yourself, you'll be gentle with others. When you're non-judgmental with yourself, you'll be non-judgmental with others. And when you give yourself the benefit of the doubt, you'll be able to do the same for the people around you, too.

Turn on the Light

The simple truth about loneliness: you can sit alone in the dark or you can get up, turn on the light, open the door and invite a friend or two in.

We all feel lonely from time to time, and everything I read and hear from other people confirms that loneliness is an epidemic. I share that with you so that you don't feel alone in your loneliness; actually, you are in good company. If you are feeling lonely, it might help to shift your focus just a bit. Do you know other people who might also be feeling this way? What could you do to help them feel less alone?

Pretend for a moment that you wanted to solve the loneliness problem for a specific friend. What are some suggestions you might have for them? Once you have a few ideas swirling around, try one or two of those for yourself. I know that when I am feeling lonely, I am also not energized or motivated to do anything about it. This is another one of those times when you have to focus less on the 'feeling,' and more on the 'doing.' And there is an added payoff here - when you become less lonely, there is a good chance someone else is less lonely, too.

Optimism Grounded in Reality

Doing our best doesn't mean we don't make mistakes. It doesn't mean that we are perfect or that everything works out the way we want in the timeframe we were planning. It doesn't mean that we don't have disappointments or that we are always smiling, always hopeful or always energized with a positive spirit. What it does mean is we know how to pick ourselves up and dust ourselves off, and we keep moving one small step at a time.

I have always emphasized the 'balanced approach' to optimism – optimism, grounded in reality keeps us moving forward while paying attention to other day-to-day realities that require and deserve attention, too.

Stepping Into the Unknown

We don't always step into the unknown with self-confidence or lack of fear. In fact, sometimes we can barely breathe, and our hands are trembling. But we do step out with a sense of self-respect, courage and belief that we deserve more. And as we move into the mystery, we discover that our courage, our faith and our self-awareness is deepening, with every single step we take.

I love this thought and it resonates with me in very real ways. I often find myself outside my comfort zone. An example: I have always wanted to take improvisation or "improv" classes. These are performances – often comedic – that have no script.

Recently I had the opportunity to enroll in a comedy club improv class and true to form, I agreed. Saying yes did not mean I was totally comfortable. In fact, I was nervous before every single class. But it was really a lot of fun and as the course progressed, I started enjoying it more and more and the nerves began to dissipate. As the experience concluded, I was proud of myself for having the courage to take a step into the unknown.

Sometimes a Detour Is a Gift

Things don't always go the way we had expected or hoped. Sometimes we work hard, stay focused and keep taking those small steps, and we still come up against a brick wall. That never feels good. It's easy to get discouraged during these moments and taking a break, a breather and a time out makes sense. It also makes sense to see if that brick wall has something to tell us that might suggest adjustments to our goal. But letting a brick wall cause you to give up would be like stopping an exciting trip because you came to a stop sign.

A short time ago, Mike and I went out to eat at one of our favorite restaurants in Orlando. I ordered skillet lasagna. It arrived and looked delicious. As I began eating, I realized there was no lasagna pasta! I mentioned it to our server who seemed puzzled and explained the chef was 82 and maybe forgot! Obviously, this was not a brick wall, but it did remind me to be patient, expect upsets, and to keep things in perspective. After discovering the missing lasagna noodles, the sever got me a side of spaghetti to go with my dinner... and a complimentary desert!

P.S. As we finished our dinner, I remembered that I had once made grape-nut pudding and forgot to add the grape-nuts!

Take a Moment to Remember

As the day unfolds, take a moment to remember the good things you already have in your life. Then with an open heart and outstretched arms, gently move into your day. As thoughts drift into your mind, carefully sort them. Those that are worthy and helpful, use to shape your actions. And those that are unworthy and hurtful gently cast aside and let them go.

I don't know why it's easier to focus on our challenges than on our blessings but, at least for me, I do find that is where my thoughts often go. It takes practice to catch yourself when you're doing that, and it takes practice to replace a focus on the negative with a focus on our blessings. With practice, you'll get better at it. And with lots of practice, you may find yourself skipping the negative thoughts, altogether.

Your Life Is an Example

Are you living your life in a way that teaches others how important it is to respect yourself and your dreams? That shows how essential it is to pursue your passions with enthusiasm and an open heart? Your example will change lives, and the people you love are watching.

If we are not treating ourselves respectfully, we are inviting disrespect from others. And if there are people in our lives, we want to teach self-respect to, the only way to do that is to practice it.

Being Real Means Being You

If we want to connect in authentic, meaningful ways with other people, we must be willing to show up as our honest selves. Otherwise, the masquerade ball will continue to swirl as we dance around the truth, and we'll miss meeting all the beautiful, loving and amazing people who surround us on the sidelines.

When I was younger, I didn't know what being 'in the closet' meant intellectually, but emotionally, I got it loud and clear. I was aware that I was somehow different, and that those differences were more of a problem – not a blessing. Like most kids, I wanted others to love me, and I quickly learned that my best hope for that would come from hiding my differences, not celebrating them. Looking back now, I realize that this decision – made by a confused and frightened little boy – missed the simple but profound truth that to be loved as me, required me to be me.

Leap of Faith

When we leap into the unknown, we discover our courageous, adventurous and hopeful selves once again. And never forget that sometimes a leap is that small step we almost decided not to take.

Your true purpose and deep potential are unfolding even as you read these words. You are on board, and the train has left the station. And although the destination may not be in full view just yet, you can be certain that as you remain open to the possibilities, the horizon will become clearer. For now, just sit back, relax and let the gentle motion of the train guide your path.

You Can Begin Again

Each morning we wake up and are handed the gift of a new day, a fresh start and a chance to begin again. It's what we do with this gift that counts.

I need to tape this to my coffee maker because I constantly need to remember this. It's such a fundamental truth that by now, I know it by heart. My only problem is my overactive mind often isn't paying attention. Try to take a gentle moment of reflection each morning and then wait to see what gifts are in store.

Growing Older Is Still Growing

The wonderful part of growing older is the growing part!

This is something I am struggling with right now. How can I grow older with grace, optimism and hope for the future? And I don't have all the answers and may never figure it all out either. On one hand, I have aches and pains, a few health issues (real and imagined) and I am slowing down. On the other hand, I am really excited about new projects, have a to-do list a mile long, and I am still dreaming new things and taking those small steps. I am thinking more and more that it's less about thinking, and more about doing. Less about knowing and more about discovering.

Kindness Begins at Home

No matter how today went, there's a very good chance you did the best you could. So be extraordinarily gentle with yourself.

It's not an original thought that we are our own worst critics, but it does bear repeating. I wonder why we are so hard on ourselves. Being gentler with ourselves starts with paying attention to when we're giving ourselves a hard time. When I am aware that I am doing that, I ask myself, "Why?" I'm not always expecting an answer but more of a transition. Smiling in recognition helps, too. Practice with me. And then practice some more.

Let Go of Judgment

All the judgments we make add up and weigh us down. And holding on to them consumes so much energy. One by one, let them fade into the rearview mirror and begin using all that energy to make the people around you feel good, valued and loved, instead.

Letting go of judgment for me is an ongoing process. It got easier as I began to pay attention to all the judging I was doing. I judged the weather, the coffee, the color of a car, the attitude of the receptionist, what television shows were good, funny, worthwhile, and on and on and on.

So, begin by noticing how many judgments you are making hour by hour, day by day. Then practice reframing the judgment. For example, the color of the car is not awful, (obviously, the person who bought the car liked the color) it's just not appealing to me. This can become a game that you can play often, and soon you will find yourself judging less, and laughing more.

You Can Feel Better

Sometimes, like a low-grade fever, we've lived with anxiety, fear, anger, or resentment for so long that we've forgotten that this isn't how we are meant to feel. If this is an issue with you, the first step is to decide you don't want to feel like this any longer. The second and more difficult step is to ask, "What would I have to do to feel better?" Your answer could be the beginning of a whole new way of life.

Many years ago, I was diagnosed with generalized anxiety disorder (GAD) and I can remember the very first time I had an anxiety attack. I can remember being terrified when I had to give a speech or make remarks in public. Being diagnosed and educating myself about anxiety helped. Therapy helped. A little book by Barry McDonagh called DARE helped.

I've come a long way, and now mostly enjoy speaking in public, doing podcasts and interviews. I still think I am diagnosable, but I am much, much better. Our mental health is so important, and like our physical health, I've never met anyone who didn't have some issue to work on. If you have something you'd like to work on, take that small step, today.

Why Perspective Matters

Every once and a while, we're bound to have a day that feels like a near disaster. Looking back, these will be remembered as 'just one of those days.' But in that moment, they can be very discouraging. At some point, we'll understand that something bigger and better was just around the corner, but for now, give in and trust that things will work out just fine.

Human beings, at least the ones I know, often have a hard time putting things in perspective. It takes time and space to really do it and I'm learning that just knowing that a healthier perspective will come with time, is enough for right now. On those disastrous days, remembering this doesn't make me feel all better, but often a little bit better. And a little bit is better than nothing!

Turn Down the Worry Dial

Are you worried about tomorrow, or are you finally learning that worry is the most overrated, unproductive pastime ever invented? If there's some small step you can take today that will improve the odds for tomorrow, take it. And if not, go for a walk or listen to some music, call a friend, see a funny movie, and count your blessings instead.

I am a worrier and a problem-solver. I am also hypervigilant, hypersensitive and intuitive, too. And honestly, these qualities are not just challenges for me; they are also gifts. They are part of me, and I don't wish them away. At the same time, sometimes enough is enough. I can't change who I am, but I can turn down the dial just a bit and that really helps me a lot. Going for a walk, reading a book, putting on some music (preferably show tunes) and cuddling with our goldendoodle Toby are just some of the ways I can change the channel.

Sometimes It's a Jigsaw Puzzle

Small steps are required to reach big goals and they add up the same way a beautiful tapestry is made up of many small threads. Your small steps will sometimes go according to plan, and other times bring us to unexpected and even more beautiful places than we had ever intended. Be comfortable with clear goals but be open to a little mystery, too.

When I begin working on a goal and taking those first few small steps, I have learned to expect that the pathway forward is almost always different than what I might have expected. So now I expect to be surprised. That said, I also believe with all my heart and soul that small steps are the way to move forward. Some days, I take a whole bunch of small steps that turn into big progress. Some days, I take a small step and hit a brick wall.

Discovering a door that won't open is just as important as finding a door that opens easily. Have you ever completed a jigsaw puzzle without trying to put pieces into place that look like a fit but aren't? Me, either. Getting to your goal will not be a slam dunk; it will be a jigsaw puzzle.

Change is Inevitable

Our growth and change are often stressful to those around us. Don't let the resistance or lack of encouragement from others slow you down. Instead, gently smile knowing that the pushback is very often a confirmation that you are making things happen, and that you're on the right track.

If you haven't had this experience, I bet you haven't tried evolving and growing while in a relationship. Change is hard enough for us in isolation, but when we're changing, those around us are often even more challenged because they're caught off guard.

Think about your own reactions to the changes those around you may have set in motion. It is unsettling at best, and often downright scary. Telling people what's going on, helps. Knowing it comes with the territory helps. One-step-at-a-time helps. Letting others who are important to you grow and evolve helps. Let those around you share your adventure and be open to sharing theirs. Change is inevitable and good and natural. Embrace it.

Take One Step Today

Lack of confidence and low self-esteem can slow us down or even keep us stuck, but don't let that stop you from taking a step today. Discover for yourself that action builds our self-esteem, and as we move forward, our confidence will grow. Take one step today, even if you don't yet believe.

Most of us, even those with a healthy sense of self-confidence, need validation. We seek it from others. We offer it to others. And we can learn to self-validate, too. Patting yourself on the back is healthy – do more of it. Give out those pats to others because they need it. To a large extent, we get to create the community that surrounds us. Be a self-esteem-builder and you will attract others who are inspired by getting and giving those pats more freely.

You Can Make Things Happen

It's easy to make excuses, but a lot more fun to make things happen.

How did we get so good at making excuses for others and for ourselves, too? When I find myself doing this, it's usually because someone wants me to do something I don't want to do, or because I should be doing something that, for all kinds of reasons, I don't care to. When it comes to pleasing others, the only real excuse you need is the truth. Practice just being honest with people. Now, when it comes to the excuses you make for <u>yourself,</u> here's a strategy that changed my life: I simply take a small step in the direction of that very thing.

Everyone Struggles

There are lots of things that don't go our way, but we still need to keep going. When we move forward with a smile and a sense of hopefulness, we are more likely to feel better and meet others who will inspire and motivate us to make important and good things happen.

It's important to remember that everyone is struggling in some invisible, or visible, way. I don't mean most people; I mean all people. It's part of being a human. If our intention is to smile and encourage each other, everyone in our lives is given a ray of hope. And a ray of hope makes smiling easier. That's a habit that makes a much bigger difference than you could possibly imagine.

Less Fear is Possible

For many of us, feeling scared has become a habit rather than a reaction to a real threat. But fortunately, we can learn a new behavior by moving forward anyway, replacing fear with feelings of bravery and power. After a while, we'll be able to skip the 'scared' part and go right to the powerful and brave feelings instead.

To be honest, I am not sure that skipping the scared part is an actual destination, but it's a trip we can take. And getting to the powerful part comes easier with practice. Here's a thought: you've actually been practicing for a long while, now. It's already easier. It can be even easier. Keep practicing.

Why Quiet Time Matters

It's amazing what you can learn when you spend some quiet time alone with yourself. And it's astonishing and profoundly sad what you'll miss when you don't. Almost every answer you need is already deep within you, and you owe it to yourself, your loved ones, and the world to discover them without further delay. You are here, and therefore, you are ready.

I am a book, already filled with information that will help me and guide me – I've just left it on the bookshelf unopened and unheard. Being by yourself with no music, no TV and no distractions is not a place always easy to find. Try a walk outside or sit in your car or lock yourself in the bathroom and let the quiet calm you down so you can remember what deep-down you already know. Then take note of what you hear.

Growing Older With Grace

What we call 'the reality of growing older' needs a little light. Let's grow older with grace, a sense of wonder, and a deep appreciation for the opportunities we have been given to grow more, create more, and be more.

Most of us tend to complain about getting older more easily that we celebrate the gift we've been given. We talk about our sore knees, health concerns, financial worries, or the body parts that are slowing down. But that talk comes easy. Thinking about and talking about this new chapter as a blessing takes a real effort but is a challenge worth taking.

Focus On Living Well

The goal is not to avoid the fears associated with an adventurous life. The goal is to be so busy living a good one, you hardly notice them.

I am a list maker and I love crossing things off my to-do list. Sometimes when I do something not on the actual list, I add it just so I can cross it off. Maybe getting things done is a coping mechanism for me. Maybe it's a mental health fitness exercise I do. All I'm sure of is if I am getting things done, I have less time to be focused on worries and fears.

I also want to give a word of encouragement to those who are discouraged and depressed and seemingly unable to get busy or stay engaged. Remember the power of small steps. I have worked with people who started by simply getting out of bed and brushing their teeth. I admire you so much for finding something small and doable. I celebrate you. I love you for what you are doing!

It's All Your Time

Please don't feel surprised or guilty because you need rest, quiet time, alone time, meditative be-still time. Saying "yes" to those essentials are just as important as making things happen.

This sounds so easy but for some of us (meaning me and some of you) this is difficult. It's easy for me to say, "Don't feel guilty or surprised," but actualizing it is a major challenge. All I can tell you is I need to remember this all the time and then I actually need to force myself to slow down and rest. If this comes easy to you, you're lucky. And you might have to remember that too much of a good thing is too much!

Being True to You

Some walks we must take by ourselves, not because we don't love or need others, but because we also need to know and love ourselves.

It can be incredibly powerful when we know and show up as ourselves. As a gay man who spent 45 years in the closet, I speak from a place of deep experience. I also can share that I discovered the closet was full, not just with gay kids, but all kinds of kids who had been taught or somehow figured out that they needed to hide part of who they were. As we learn to know and love ourselves more, we open ourselves up to be known and loved by others. It's likely a lifetime process and as we know and love ourselves more and more, we invite others to do the same.

You're Perfectly Imperfect

You – and all the things in your life – are perfectly imperfect. So don't wait until the stars are perfectly aligned to take a small step towards your dream. There is no day like today, and no time like right now.

We never look into a night sky and see the exact same sky as we saw the night before. The stars are always evolving and changing and how they are aligned right now, is perfect for right now. Remember that waiting for something to happen before taking a small step is an excuse. It's a stall tactic. Don't fall for it.

Small Things Can Be Game Changers

Sure, we're vulnerable, and even needy sometimes. But even then, we each have the capacity and power to get outside of ourselves to comfort and encourage others. Today, keep your eyes open for an opportunity to help someone, and create a day that enriches both of you.

Some of the most encouraging and inspiring people in the world are those who just came out of a storm. They may be exhausted and stunned but when they make eye contact with us, when they manage a small smile or nod, they are shifting the universe in life altering ways. I want to be like them.

Focus On Gratitude and Joy

When we focus on all the things we don't have, we miss the opportunity to appreciate, be grateful for, and enjoy all that we do have.

We can make a list of all the things that are wrong in our lives and our world, our worries and regrets, and things that scare us or overwhelm us. Or we can make a list of things we are grateful for. Both lists can be honest ones, but one will lift us up. Which one will you choose?

Find Meaning in Purpose

You are here on purpose.

I used to believe that we had one primary purpose in life that I referred to as "our north star." I now realize that we have multiple purposes. And if you're wondering about your purposes, one big purpose we all share is simply understanding that we are here to find meaning in our lives. If we don't feel a lot of meaning, that doesn't mean it isn't there, it just means we need to dig a little deeper. For me, I have found meaning in what I have to offer the people in my world. If you're on a quest for meaning, start there and play with it. If you do that, I can promise that you are already on the right path.

You're Still Here!

When you are feeling fearful, tense, worried, or stuck, just remember – you've been here before and you've always worked your way through it. You are so much stronger and so much more capable than you give yourself credit for. Just look at all you've already dealt with and remind yourself – you're still here! And with that realization, find the courage and tenacity to take that next small step.

You are already a survivor. You've already completed so many races, won so many blue ribbons, and proven your resilience many times over. I sometimes need to be reminded of this. I need to remember how many challenges I have faced and survived. When I remember what I have already done, the next small steps aren't as intimidating, and I am less likely to put them off. When I remember what I have already accomplished, I actually am more hopeful about what I will do next.

Be Gentle with Yourself

As you recall your personal setbacks and disappointments, be gentle with yourself. You did the best you could then, and through these experiences you've been learning, growing and getting better. Tomorrow is a new day, and there will be plenty of opportunities to begin again.

I am not sure where the need to find someone to blame comes from, but for most of us, when we're feeling down, we begin the search. And often, the first person we blame is ourselves. More and more, I see setbacks and disappointments as just part of how life goes, and I try to take responsibility when it makes sense, but also try and remember that mistakes are more often like catching a cold... sometimes things just happen!

Let People In

If you've spent most of your life trying to get people to *like* you, consider spending the rest letting them get to *know* you.

This is not just one of your greatest challenges, it's also one of your all-time greatest opportunities. The more of 'you' that's shared, the more of you there is to really love. People aren't really drawn to perfect people; they're drawn to real people. I understand that you may have been hurt or may have had poor role models, and some of your behaviors may need to be worked on, but part of sharing the real you involves doing the work to uncover the real you.

It's Your Turn

Many of us are learning how to speak up and speak clearly about what we need and what's important to us. When we do, we are often surprised to discover that people actually do hear us and respond appropriately. And if they don't, at least we've done our best to communicate and we can feel better about doing what's right for our own emotional well-being. And even more important, we can be certain the universe heard every single word.

Why do we have so much difficulty speaking our truths? Part of the answer is we haven't spent much time listening to ourselves and we have lost touch with who we are, what we want and what we need. I suspect that it's a well-intentioned but quite misguided, learned behavior. This gets really complicated in all kinds of relationships when both parties are both out of touch and unable to speak directly and clearly. The more you practice, the more you listen, the easier it gets.

Find Comfort Outside Your Zone

Often when we make the decision to step into the unknown and take a chance on our dreams, we feel vulnerable, unsure of ourselves, lonely, and even scared. And we wonder if we made a mistake or should turn back. These are the feelings that come with every great adventure, so stay strong. Excitement, joy, feelings of soaring and self-confidence are just around the corner.

I have never done anything creative, outside of my comfort zone, or big without feeling scared. I have learned to expect it and see it as confirmation that I am growing, again. I've also learned that feeling scared is a close cousin to feeling excited. Sometimes I can't tell them apart.

Share the Real You

One of the most self-affirming and self-respectful things you can do is to stand up for yourself and what you believe in. In other words, be real with the people you care about. And at the end of the day if that costs you a few acquaintances or even friendships, consider it 'spring cleaning' and a life-changing step toward authenticity.

To be real with you is an honor and a privilege, and I hope you feel the same. In some strange and wonderful way, even though most of us haven't actually met, we do know each other. And the more time we spend together, the more we each learn about ourselves, our lives, and our triumphs and disappointments, too. Good days and not-so-good days are all part of real lives. Knowing that is comforting, because we want to be real and because we remember we are not alone.

Why the Next Step Matters

Moving forward despite our fears and obstacles is one of the most difficult, most empowering, and lifechanging things we will ever do.

Feeling scared is a very common, understandable feeling when we are faced with challenges or threats. In fact, feeling scared is a very rational response to danger, either real or imagined. If it's real, we can't be immobilized because we actually need to take steps to protect ourselves. If it's imagined, we also can't become immobilized because then we are giving up our ability to power through a feeling that's not based in reality. Always remember you can feel the fear and be powerful at the same time. You have been scared a million times before and you have always found your way through every situation that has come your way.

A Glimmer of Hope

If you've reached a place where you're not feeling a lot of hope, take a small step towards achieving a goal or solving a problem or challenge, anyway. Once you do, you will begin to remember how powerful you really are, and you'll begin to feel a little more hopeful. Soon you'll be feeling a lot more hopeful, and that's when you'll know you have turned another corner.

I have discovered that having a little hope sometimes starts with something as simple as just a desire. Wanting it is actually the beginning of having it, even if it's just an acknowledgment. And then keep your eyes and heart open, because it's closer than you think.

Now What?

Some of the most amazing people in our lives have been discouraged and hurt. They have had their hearts broken, and their hopes dashed. They have missed opportunities, had regrets, and made mistakes. Their lives have not always been easy or perfect. They have endured sadness and worry and have been confused and alone. And these very same people have gotten up each morning on the good days and the not-so-good-days too, gotten dressed and asked themselves "Now what?" And the answer to that question has taken them to some beautiful, incredible, and wonderful places.

"Now what?" is a question I ask myself almost every day. Sometimes it's about little upsets or opportunities, and other times it comes from a place of pain and confusion. I almost always get an answer, and usually the answer is another small step. I rarely have breakthrough answers. More often it's a 'next step' idea that keeps me moving.

Leaning into the Good

There will always be people who are more than happy to tell you what's wrong with you, your life and the world. I suggest spending more time with those people who focus on what's good, and what's right with your life. More often than not, they'll be the very same people with ideas that will help you move forward. And no doubt, you will have an idea or two to share with them, too.

One of our most underutilized powers is the power we have to decide who to spend time with. The older I get, the more powerful I become, and I use that power to be around people who want me to be happy and at peace. Usually, this doesn't mean you have to leave people who aren't cheering you on. It more often means you just choose to spend more time with people who are.

Swim with the Current

Sometimes, when we feel that we are being tossed about in random, powerful, and meaningless currents, what's actually happening is a life-changing course correction. Stay hopeful and strong.

Sometimes we must just sit with not knowing. And sometimes we must decide if we are just postponing the inevitable because we are afraid and recognize that it's time to act. And there are other times when sitting or pausing is just the right thing to do. If you're not sure which is which, take a moment to pause for a short while, and then check back in. Talk with a trusted friend or therapist. Journal. Go for long walks. You will eventually know when it's time for action.

Learn to Forgive

As we forgive ourselves, we are learning the art of forgiveness.

I am not sure I know the path for the self-forgiveness journey. For me, it seems to happen in bits and pieces. The more I own the responsibility for my mistakes and try and make amends when I can, the easier it gets to be gentle with myself. And ironically, the kinder and more forgiving I am toward myself, the kinder more forgiving I am able to be for others.

It's Not Your Job

Obviously, we are called to love, help, support and encourage other people. But one very common mistake many of us make is trying to make someone else (or everyone else) happy. It just can't be done. Instead, we need to turn our attention to our own goals and dreams and the things that we feel passion for. By doing this, we teach others by example how to seek happiness for themselves.

I can tell you that this is one I am still working on. I seem intent on always trying to 'fix' people so they can be happier and more hopeful and excited about their lives. So far, I've been more successful at helping by example than by fixing. In fact, when it comes to fixing, I have had zero success. But I am still a work in progress, too, and I learn every day.

The Beauty of a Snowflake

If you can find real joy in little things, then you have begun to understand miracles.

We are surrounded by tiny miracles. A cup of coffee, a stranger's smile, the sunrise, a gentle rain, cats and dogs, babies, flowers, laughter, and love. The more we look, the more we can see.

Feeling Alone

Even when we feel all alone, we are surrounded by light.

I believe in an invisible force field of goodness. It goes by many different names, and it's mostly indescribable. Sometimes it's not easy to see or feel, but it's aways there. On a cloudy day, is the sun still there? The answer to that question is the same answer. It's always there.

A Funny Thing

We may not be perfect, and we often make mistakes. Sometimes we even get sidetracked. But we are also moving forward, one step at a time, and that beats giving up or staying stuck any day.

Part of moving forward involves wrong turns, missteps, and detours. If we let fear of these things stop us, we stay stuck. When we accept that they come with the territory, we keep moving. And a funny thing I have noticed is what I first thought was a wrong turn, has frequently led to some pretty amazing things. I have also met some incredible people who have changed my life in some of those unexpected places. Sometimes mistakes are just unfortunate mistakes, and other times they are incredible adventures. Accept the unfortunate ones, and keep your eyes peeled for the incredible ones down the road.

Not Everyone Likes Me

You can be certain that not everyone will like the short story you wrote, the cake you baked, the painting you created, the way you dress, or the choices you make. But you can be equally certain that most of these very same people would give anything to have your passion. And if they were honest with themselves, they'd admit they'd like to be engaged and making life happen, just like you.

With almost every post I make on my public social media pages, someone doesn't agree. If I wanted only 100% positive feedback on my work, I wouldn't show up each day. Yes, I seek out people who like what I do, but I often learn something from the people who don't. It's kind of a win-win situation. That said, I still prefer to hang out with people who encourage and appreciate me.

It's Just Around the Corner

Stay strong. You're closer than you think.

As long as I am moving and taking those small steps, I figure I am getting closer. That doesn't mean that I don't need to rest and restore, but it does mean I can keep my eye on the goal and keep moving. This is true for small goals, like packing for a trip, and big goals, like writing a book. There are so many corners; I wonder what's around the next one!

Shift Your Focus to Action

There are body slams, soul slams and heart slams, too. We can have the wind knocked out of us by unemployment, relationship transitions, financial pressures, and all sorts of unexpected and sometimes terrifying scenarios. By now, we have learned that life is not always gentle, or that moving on, or even getting up and out of bed, is always easy. But we've also learned that when times are tough, we need to shift our focus to action. That's when we find one small thing we can do and do it. Then find another small thing, and then another. It's the pathway to better times.

Most of us, myself included, know what body, heart and soul slams are. We've all had them, and somehow, we have survived. The small action steps I often talk about are not just the right things to do, often they're the only thing we can do. So, we get out of bed, we brush our teeth, find a book to read, plan something for dinner, do a load of laundry or watch a funny TV show. Small steps may be tiny, but when we're moving, we are still in the game and, truth be told, sometimes that's the only way to move beyond those slams. I know you can do it because like me, you've done it before.

If I Had a Million Dollars

It's time for us to get serious about the passions we've been given. If your passions are buried deep, start digging. If we see them clearly, get moving. And if we're already moving, why not pick up the pace a bit? The truth is, being able to take that next small step is an incredible gift.

'Passion' is an emotional and powerful word. It's so emotional and powerful that it can sometimes scare us. And sometimes, for a million different reasons, we forget what our passions are. Uncovering them takes work and time. We can begin by simply asking ourselves for clues. What did I like as a child? What did I want to do when I grew up? What natural gifts do I have? What's my idea of fun? If I had a million dollars, what would I do? Invite other people to suggest clues, too. What do they see in you that you might not be able to see for yourself? I have grown to believe we aren't given just one passion or one purpose, either. We are always evolving and growing and becoming, and now is a good time to check in and begin to uncover gifts you may be ignoring.

I majored in art when I started college. I felt this passion around creating and thought that meant I should draw or paint. I also wanted to be an actor and I tried that a bit, too. In both instances, I learned that I wasn't particularly gifted at it, but it propelled me to discover another outlet – writing. So, I paint with words now.

You Deserve Love

You deserve to be loved, and you can begin by loving yourself.

I can't tell you exactly how to love yourself. I think it's different for each of us. When I feel I need to show myself a little love, I try imagining what that might look like for someone else. Taking a third-person perspective sometimes makes it easier for us to uncover what it is we need. Some general ideas include listening to ourselves, letting ourselves feel sad or angry, crying, or laughing. It also includes treating yourself with respect and putting some boundaries in place so others will recognize the difference, too.

Remember, it's not just 'okay' to pay attention to your own needs – it's essential. An undernourished heart and soul have so much less to offer the rest of the world (including family, friends, co-workers and strangers) than hearts and souls that are filled. So, learn to take care of yourself. The rest of the world needs you fully charged.

I Am Here!

The best way to speak up for yourself is by taking action steps that say, "I am here! I have a dream and I am moving forward, starting right now."

*Sometimes I need to remind myself that **I am here**. I need to remember that I am not a placeholder; I am a participant. I need to remember that I deserve a meaningful life and that my dreams count. And when I remember, I take a small step and declare my space in the universe. Deep down, I believe I am here on purpose, for a purpose.*

Put Your Worries Aside

Remember that most people have had difficult challenges, loss, fear or heartbreak. Most people know how you feel because they've been there, too – usually more than once. And since these challenges are never solved with worry, let's for the moment put our worries aside and consider the possibility that everything will eventually work itself out.

Then go for a walk, watch a funny movie, talk with positive friends, take a long bath, read a good book, have a glass of wine, a cupcake, or whatever is safe and works for you, and banish every worrisome thought at least for a few minutes. You so deserve it.

Just because something is real doesn't mean it commands or deserves all our attention. I've wasted so many hours, days – probably even months and years – focused on the pain and reality I was facing, not realizing that I could own it without it owning me. So go to a funny movie. Read a mystery. Spend time with friends and cut yourself some slack. What you are going through is a very real event, but it doesn't define you unless you let it.

A Mind Shift Trick

When you find yourself feeling troubled, anxious, overwhelmed or sad, think of something you're grateful for and say it out loud. Repeat as needed.

This kind of mind shift takes practice. I tend to be a worrier, so my tendency is to lay in bed at night and easily find something to worry about. I am very good at worrying. I have been practicing shifting the conversation in my head from worrying to being grateful. Often, I begin remembering things I am grateful for, and then things briefly shift. I haven't mastered this perfectly yet, but I know that every minute I spend feeling grateful is one less minute of worrying.

Follow the Signs

What you may not yet know is that you have a very important purpose here on earth, and you have not yet accomplished all that you are called to do. Don't worry, your work is tied directly to your passion and will be fulfilling, meaningful and grounded in love. All you need to do right now is to stay open for signs that will point you in the right direction.

I should add, "If you see a sign, follow it!" Have you ever been at a stop light and not noticed when the light turned green until someone honks their horn? I have, and more often than I'd like to admit. It's good to wait patiently for the light to change, and then it also makes sense to move ahead when the light turns green.

Roadblocks and Doorways

The funny thing about setbacks and roadblocks is that very often they actually turn out to be windows and doorways. Trusting that opportunities are waiting for us makes them easier to discover.

Today might be a good day to walk a mile in your own shoes. In other words, give yourself credit for your resiliency. When you do, you'll discover a brave and tenacious person who has gotten through so much, learned so much, and given so much. Be grateful for your journey, and hopeful about what's around the next corner.

Important Work

There are many people who have been deeply wounded in their lives. Sometimes they are the people who assume the worst, who find ways to discredit or bring others down, who instinctively discourage rather than encourage, who resent the success of friends and strangers, and who gossip and share negativity every chance they get. They have important and very personal work to do. In the meantime, do not let their toxicity bring you down or slow you down. You have important dreams to pursue and must always invite light and positive people to share the journey with you.

Unfortunately, there are people in our lives who are toxic. If you don't have at least one now, I bet you have had one or two in the past and somehow, figured your way free. If this is a current issue for you, if possible, get some physical distance from that person or the people who bring you down. And if distance isn't possible, refocus your energy, as best you can, in the direction of taking care of yourself and getting on with your life.

This can be a real challenge and you may need help, sometimes from a friend or mentor who can guide you. Other times, however, you might need the counsel from a therapist or coach. But whatever it takes, it will be worth it. You do have important work to do, and the first order of business might just be creating that distance.

Managing Others

It's not our job to change anyone else, and the truth is that 'fixing' others is almost always an excuse not to focus on our own growth. Changing others never works and holds us back from living our own lives with passion and enthusiasm. Redirect this energy and make something good happen today.

Have you ever been successful at fixing someone? I know I haven't and believe me I have tried my darndest. If we can agree that it doesn't work, then our new problem turns to discovering what to do with all that time and energy that has been focused on someone else. The answer, of course, is to make something meaningful – and even fun – happen in our own lives.

Difficult Days

We are not always guaranteed perfect, or even easy days. In fact, some of the most optimistic people I know have dealt with some extraordinary challenges and endured many dark times. So don't think easy days are always a good way to judge progress or success. Getting up and out the door on those difficult days and taking a step forward despite the challenges is a much more accurate barometer.

I was talking about anxiety on a podcast recently. I shared that almost every morning I wake up with a free-floating, nonspecific sense of anxiety. I have learned that as soon as I get out of bed, put the coffee on, feed our dog, Toby, and begin my day, the anxiety slowly begins to dissipate. In other words, taking those simple and small steps creates an energy shift for me. The host of the podcast shared that she has a similar experience, and perhaps some readers do as well. The real message here is to figure out what helps you get out the door, and then do more of that.

Be a Wave in a Mighty Ocean

We have all had times when the simple act of putting one foot in front of the other has taken every last ounce of energy we could muster. That's why we need good people and positive messages around us to encourage us through these difficult times. And when we take turns giving and receiving, we all benefit.

I believe that we are each a wave in a mighty ocean, and as our positive thoughts and actions join with our fellow waves, miracles begin, the world changes and our life begins to unfold with grace and passion. The tide goes out, and the tide comes in. Some days the ocean is rough, and other days it's peaceful and calm.

Just Do It

Today, don't ponder. Don't hesitate or worry about the outcome, what others will think, or whether it makes sense or not. Just take a small step towards something important to you.

Hopefully, this thought will encourage you to take a meaningful step forward somewhere – even if you are uncertain. Being hesitant is often just an excuse to stay stuck. And even if your small step turns out to be a misstep, it's only a small one and you'll learn so much in the process.

Gifts with Responsibility

The simple, yet not always popular, truth is that you are responsible for your own life. What you do, and who you become is up to you. That's a wonderful responsibility and a tremendous gift, and all the more reason to make today count.

At the end of the day, this is a difficult lesson to learn but a powerful one, too. You do have an incredible amount of power to make your life a life you want, but the only way I know to discover our power is to understand that it's up to us. If there's something I want to have happen in my life, I have learned that there are two essential follow-up questions that need to be asked: "What must I do to make that happen?" and, "Am I willing to do what needs to be done?" Then I can decide which of these things is genuinely worth the time and effort to take those next important steps.

Action Matters

What we say, think and feel is extremely important. But what we *do*, matters more. Do one small thing to acknowledge and enliven your passion today. It will count.

At any point in time, we have choices to make. Are we going to dream about it, or are we going to do something about it? Are we going to be stuck, or are we going to get moving? These are not just choices; they are game changers. What are you going to do?

Getting Through Difficult Days

Sometimes during difficult days, all we can do is put one foot in front of the other. The good news is that one morning we'll wake up and understand how strong we really are, how far along we've traveled, and how much better things have become.

You already know this because you have experienced it. Small steps are relatively easy to take. It's hard to come up with a believable or credible excuse for not taking it. And we know that small steps do add up – sometimes slower and other times faster than we expect. And sometimes I experience the small steps as skipping. And it's hard to take just one skip.

Make Something Happen!

Today belongs to you. Don't worry so much about what might or might not happen. Instead make something small actually happen. Choose power over powerlessness and begin to move forward.

A while back I learned that I spent a lot of time wringing my hands about things that I didn't have any power over. For example, I might worry about the weather on a day I was attending an outdoor concert. At the same time, I didn't use the power I did have to find my raincoat and umbrella just in case the weather got wet. I may not have the power to make everything or everyone feel perfect, but I do have the power to remain optimistic and hopeful in ways that may inspire others to feel more at peace, too.

It's Not Too Late

Time passes so quickly. If you hear a voice saying your dreams should wait, don't listen.

It's never too late to get started on some version of a dream we might have. Recently I spoke at a local book club and an 82-year-old woman who had always wanted to play the piano went home that night and scheduled her first lesson. That made me very happy. The small step process allows you to work on your dreams, no matter how much else you have going on. Remember how fast time passes, and now (at least for me) it seems to go faster with each passing year.

Breathe

Every storm cloud passes. Every single one.

I know you have what it takes to get through the storm, but that doesn't mean what it takes isn't heavy and exhausting! Rest when you can, and let others help if they're around and able. Sometimes I imagine I have to manage the storm all by myself when I am surrounded by people willing to help. And sometimes the people willing to help are more capable and competent when it comes to managing a particular storm. You want to be there for others, so why not let others be there for you?

A Stumble or a Waltz?

Sometimes that small step forward feels more like a stumble. Just remember that even a stumble is action, and action beats being stuck any day.

When I was younger, I wanted to be an actor. I started going to auditions for commercials in Boston and given that I had no experience or training, I wasn't very good at it. And sometimes I ended up feeling embarrassed because I was so far out of the league. Sometimes the casting directors were really looking for a 'type' or a 'look' and being talented wasn't that important. One day the stars happened to align and I got the part. This entire acting journey had so many stumbles, but I continued to show up each day, did the work, and I was rewarded. I was an actor!

A Pebble in a Pond

Even though we will probably never know the specific ripple effects of a kind word, a gentle touch, a smile, a handful of coins, or a note of encouragement, we can be certain that our small and kind gestures are making the world a sweeter place.

There have been many days when a small or kind gesture has not only changed my mood, but it has also changed my day. I've gone from grouchy to friendly just because the person selling me a donut (I know I should probably say fruit smoothie!) smiled and called me "Sweetie." And because my mood shifted, everyone I came in contact with from that point forward had a chance to have their mood shifted, too. I like to imagine a powerful 'simple kindness pandemic.' Who knows how many fights with partners, car accidents, or missed opportunities were avoided simply because of that one sweet experience of mine?

All the Proof You Need

When we are feeling fearful, tense, worried or stuck, we just need to remember we've been here before and we've always worked our way through it. We are so much stronger and so much more capable than we may think. And if you don't believe me, just look at all you've already dealt with and remind yourself, "I'm still here."

You are resilient and you have the history, the wounds, the scars and the memories that are all the proof you need. In the introduction you may remember that I said, "I know you, and because of that I can reassure you right now that you will get past whatever is slowing you down." You will, because you always have.

Less About Why and More About How

Is there something you've been putting off for days, weeks or even years? Instead of figuring out why, use today to take a step (small steps always count) to set it in motion. In other words, move it from your to-do list to your make-it-happen list. One small step is all it takes and there's no time like now.

Here's a question I ask myself all the time: "What do you want and what are you willing to do today to begin making it happen?" And so far, when I've asked and taken time to listen, I've always figured out something I could do. That's how my first book got written, how I improved my credit score, and how I finally met a new friend who has made my world better and brighter. I have had some really big dreams come true, not overnight, but by taking one small step and then another. I also think by taking those small steps you create space for fate, luck, and the kindness of others to help.

Today Belongs to You

Today belongs to those who claim it. That doesn't mean everything will go your way, but it does mean you are committed to taking at least one small step towards resolving a challenge or moving forward on a dream. Claim this day, because it's invigorating and because the life you want and deserve depends on it.

Seize the day. Carpe Diem. What more do I need to say?

You're OK, Really

Sometimes we need to cut ourselves a little slack. We need to accept that missteps, mistakes and decisions that didn't work out the way we had hoped are just part of life. We need to remember that we are human and not created or expected to be worry-free, happy, or optimistic all the time. And, finally, we need to remember there's another part of being human that allows us to feel hopeful even when things look and feel hopeless. That's our resiliency.

Here's a game changer: it's important to be kind to others, but let's also be kind to ourselves. If I focused on all my regrets and mistakes, I wouldn't have much time left to focus on what I wanted to have happen or what lessons I've learned. Our history and all the wrong turns have actually shaped us and gotten us to where we are right now. And where you are right now is the perfect place to begin heading where you want to go. There was a book I read a long time ago that really stayed with me. It was called, "I'm OK - You're OK." Let's start with that as our new mantra and accept what has been. Then, let's get on with our lives.

A Promise

Just as the sun always returns, even after many stormy days, you will get to that better place sometime soon. That's a promise.

As I read this, I am reminded that 'soon' is relative, and sometimes it's farther away than we'd like. The truth is, I am not an expert, but I can share my experience. I am convinced that the sun will return, and my wish is that you catch a glimpse of light and feel the warmth soon.

Worrying Does Not Protect Us

The practice of worrying is a powerful and seductive habit. Many of us believe that worrying somehow protects us or is a price we must pay. But worrying never really helps and always makes us feel anxious and powerless. Instead, we need to give ourselves permission to think of or do something that makes us feel less anxious, and even happier. Sure, it takes practice, but it's time now to begin practicing habits that bring light and lightness into our lives.

For what it's worth, the quote you just read is an excerpt from my life's story. If it resonates with you, then you and I have a lot in common. Consider this your official invitation to practice new habits with me. I can assure you that recovery is gradual and maybe not ever complete, but progress is possible. I am living proof!

You Are Here on Purpose

Beyond a shadow of a doubt, you are here on purpose. Beyond a shadow of a doubt, you have gifts to share and lives to change. Beyond a shadow of a doubt, the best place to start is with one small step towards that place which your inner voice beckons towards. It's time.

'Beyond a shadow of a doubt' doesn't leave much room for discussion. And all I can really add to this is a deep and sincere belief that you are holding this book and reading this thought because it's a moment in your life where you needed this reminder. You could prove me wrong by standing still, or you could prove me right by taking one small step. If you decide to wait, that's fine, too. You'll find your way back to this moment another day, soon.

Intentions Actually Count

Rest deeply and awake lovingly.

This is one journey you will have to discover for yourself, but I can tell you that it begins with an intention. And as an intention, you need to remind yourself over and over that this is a quest you have begun. When you get into bed, say to yourself, "I intend to sleep deeply." And when you wake up, say to yourself, "I intend to awake lovingly." Just doing this very simple thing is a beginning, and honest intentions will help create a gentle shift.

Remember and Smile

You're pretty amazing because after all you've been through, you're still standing! And with each small step forward through the difficult times, you're beginning to understand that you are stronger, more tenacious and more powerful than you ever thought. And tonight, as that undeniable truth sinks in, remember who you really are, and smile.

Who are you? My guess is that you are a kind and good person. You care about other people. You have dreams you'd like to realize, and things you want to get done. You want to grow more, learn more and do more. You want to really take hold of the gifts you've been given, and you want to have things be a little easier and a bit less stressful. This is all within your reach if you have faith and an appreciation of all it has taken to get this far.

Things Will Be Okay

Sometimes we stumble. Sometimes we can't see the light at the end of the tunnel. Sometimes we even feel like giving up. But, at the end of the day, we know that's just not who we are, and we smile and know we will get through this and that things will be okay.

Over the years, I've developed a sense that I will get through the challenges and stumbles. Of course, it doesn't always make it easy, or pain-free. Some of the challenges I have faced more recently have proven that I still can feel rattled, confused, frightened and sad. But knowing it will one day pass has been enough for me to stay hopeful and believe that I will get to safe ground eventually.

Pebbles and Mountains

You do not have to move mountains today. Start with a pebble or two. Stay focused on the small stones and the mountain-moving will take care of itself.

I have had a lot of big dreams and a few seemingly-borderline-impossible goals over the years. My experience is that shifting to finding one thing I can do today, delivers more progress. I don't think my obsession with the power of small steps is just good advice, it's more of an appreciation for how things happen and how things get done.

My partner and I recently planned a 24-hour cross-country driving trip. Step one was to get in the car. Step two, we started the engine. Step three, we drove out of the driveway, and so forth. Each mile got us closer and each mile counts. And we'd never get there at all unless we took small steps. And the beautiful part was the journey and taking it bit by bit. And, especially, taking the time to enjoy the scenery.

You've Got This

As we take steps in new directions, we can expect all kinds of feelings that slow us down or even stop us in our tracks. One of those feelings is fear. And here's something kind of revolutionary about being afraid: often what we call and recognize as fear is actually excitement! And it's a lot more fun to be excited than it is to be afraid.

You are a lot more powerful than what scares you. You have things to do, and places to go and you don't have time to be sidetracked by fear. You've got this.

Encouraging Words

If you knew how important it was to offer words of encouragement and hope to family and friends, you wouldn't go to bed without picking up the phone or sending an email or text. The ripple effect of even the simplest act of thoughtfulness is often profound, sometimes even life-changing and always, always more powerful than you think.

Being a source of encouragement is good for you. Helping someone else feel a bit better, makes you feel a bit better. Reminding people that they are resilient and not alone, reminds you that you are resilient and not alone. Cheering someone else up, cheers you up. This is powerful stuff and no matter how you're doing or how you're feeling – shifting the focus to helping someone else catch a glimmer of hope guarantees you'll see a glimmer, too. Do it because you can. Do it because it makes a difference. Do it because it's good for everyone!

Feel the Magic

There is something magical, miraculous, and beautiful happening behind the scenes of your life. If you can't sense it yet, begin to imagine it. If you can't imagine it, invite your heart and mind to open so you can begin to envision it.

The fact that you are reading this message is really all the proof you need to know beautiful things are happening for you beneath the surface. I would bet that you are sensing something good is brewing, too. You may not know what or when or where, but on some level, you know it too. And if I am wrong about your ability to feel this, let me feel it for you. I've had some experience in magical, miraculous happenings. You can trust me on this.

Moments that Find Us

There are pivotal reflection moments that find us because we were looking for an opportunity to grow, or they find us unexpectedly because we just hadn't figured out we were ready for something new to come into our lives. We are evolving and growing and becoming and sometimes that can be easy and sometimes it comes with a little pain. But either way, when it finds us, we can be assured that something meaningful and good is ahead.

One of my most important walks of my life was by the ocean where I grew up. My kids were grown, I had recently 'come out' as gay to close friends and family, and I was thinking about the rest of my life. This was the first time in a while when I was alone, quiet, calm and open to listening to my inner voice. And that afternoon I made a list of several things I wanted to have happen in my life, including a couple realistic goals, and a couple that seemed to be a bit of a reach, too. That afternoon I decided if any of my dreams were going to come true, I would need to take things up a notch. And that's when I began taking those small steps. I eventually reached those goals - even the impossible ones. I suspect you could come up with a dream or two, and I hope you'll be taking one of those solo walks yourself, soon.

The Doorway to Hope

We each have our own challenges and difficult days. But even on our darkest days, our instinct is to feel grateful for the things that we do have, and for the things that are going well. And since gratitude is the doorway to hope, we find the strength and the will to take one small step that will direct us to better and easier times. It's the human spirit at its best. It's who we are.

A while back someone sent me a thought-provoking note wondering why I was so positive all the time. They asked, "What drugs are you on?" I suspect this was a new friend who had not yet spent enough time in my motivational community to know that I have walked paths that have been extraordinarily difficult.

Most of us have had losses, heartbreak, physical challenges, illnesses, toxic relationships, major disappointments and personal challenges of every type and color. We really do understand that not everything is perfect, easy or fun all the time. But we are also tenacious good people, and we have hope, faith, and a willingness to roll up our sleeves, even when we're scared, depressed or feeling powerless. Sure, we've had to dust ourselves off a few times but we're still here and doing our best. And isn't that something, all by itself, to feel positive about?

Best Friends Forever

From this day forward, strive to be your own best friend. Look within for your dreams, your inspiration, and your sense of hope. Trust your intuition and your passion. Celebrate your strengths and be open to areas of potential growth. Believe in yourself and remember that you not only deserve a fulfilled life, but you are also exactly what the world needs.

I love live theater, especially musicals. When I see a performance, I can get lost in the moment but on some level what I truly appreciate is the miracle of how so many things come together. The playwright, the musicians, the actors and set designers, the ushers, the makeup artists, and the list goes on. I believe we are all like a Broadway musical. Our lives, our experiences, our mistakes, our pain, our joy and happy and sad tears our hopes, our gifts, our passion our hidden hopes – everything about us is coming together in a way that makes us feel alive and passionate and hopeful, while being exactly what the universe wants and needs us to be.

Mistakes Become Lessons

When we decide to let our mistakes become *lessons*, rather than regrets, we ascend into a more powerful and more logical place to view and live our lives.

If you don't have a list of regrets, I would be inclined to think you haven't lived a very real or authentic life. Living our lives is a process that unfolds as we are learning how to do it better and that ensures there will also be mistakes and missteps. We aren't given an instruction book on perfection at the onset and although most missteps or mistakes create an opportunity to grow, the mistakes we have made can feel very heavy.

If you are feeling some of that weight, what you can do is be honest with yourself, not only about where you missed the mark, but also what you learned from that experience and how your behavior moving forward has or will change. This learning and changing is also a work in progress and if you are just beginning the learning and changing part, good for you! You've taken a giant leap forward.

Amazing, Not Perfect

Through challenging times you've learned how to pick yourself up, dust yourself off and begin again. And not only that, sometimes you actually make it look like dancing. You are, in a word, *amazing*.

Amazing doesn't mean 'perfect.' Not even close. My favorite shirt can be amazing; it's soft, worn, comfortable, missing a button on a sleeve, and somehow both comfortable and comforting. When I wear it, I feel like myself. I am not a good dancer, but I dance better when I am comfortable. And when I am really comfortable, I think I become a pretty good dancer! All this to say, you deserve to be comfortable, and you deserve to be dancing a little more. Think of your favorite shirt, and then listen for the beat!

Walk on the Wild Side

As we step into the unknown, we discover that we can be fragile and strong, terrified, and brave all at the same time.

I once had a therapist who taught me something very important. Two things can be true at exactly the same time. For example: your partner really loves you, and he or she may not be good for you. Your best friend may need your support, and you may not have the resources he really needs. You may feel and be fragile, and you are also strong and competent. It can be confusing to have these mixed messages, but that's how life is. When we recognize and learn to accept this, it can help alleviate stress and confusion and empower you to continue to travel forward.

A Deeper Place

When things are going great, it's easy to send out good energy to the people around us. But even when things are challenging and worrisome, we still have good energy to share. Of course, it may mean we have to dig a little deeper, but when it comes from a deeper place it's that much more powerful.

When I am needing to dig a little deeper, I don't always do it. That doesn't mean I couldn't, it just means I decided I wouldn't. If this were a test, I wouldn't get an 'A.' I might be lucky to get a 'B' and some days maybe just a 'C+.' The point isn't so much what I do, it's remembering what I am capable of doing, and doing that more often than not. And like most things which need to come from a deeper place, the impact is deeper for the recipient of your good energy and actually for you, too.

Changing Your World

Be the first to throw a small stone of kindness into your pond and watch the ripples of love begin to change the world.

When someone is kind to me, it changes my sense of reality. I feel lighter, happier, grateful and more hopeful. And when I am feeling those things, I am just naturally kinder to others, and I presume that the person feels all of that and is kind in return. We have the simple power to change the world in this very simple, yet enormous way.

Opportunities Everywhere

If you really understood how powerful and beautiful you really are, you'd be making better things happen in your life and smiling at a lot more at strangers, too.

If you don't feel your power, turn your attention to all the things surrounding you that you can influence, change, and improve. You have the power to change someone's entire day with a kind word, a smile or a gentle touch. You can help someone who is hungry or lonely or scared with very small, deliberate actions. You will absolutely change your own day, and even your life, by focusing on what you can do. And you can begin right now.

Bridge Over Troubled Waters

Sometimes we need a bridge, and sometimes we are the bridge. There are times in our lives when we could use a little help, and other times when we are given the chance to be that help for someone else. It really doesn't matter where you are, right now. What matters is that you remember we are stronger together, and taking a hand is just as important as offering one.

As I have gotten older, I have become more comfortable sharing my joys and struggles with close friends. It's much easier spreading the joy and more helpful when I share the struggles. I spent most of my life taking care of others instead of taking care of myself and I have been consciously trying to change my ways. When I need a bridge, it's getting easier asking and letting someone be that for me. One of the beautiful ironies has been that being real gives others permission to be real. And when two people can be real, their relationship deepens in wonderful ways.

Uncomfortable, Not Unbearable

We all have experienced hurts and sorrow, heartbreak and betrayal. There is no way to sugarcoat those experiences and no need to, either. During tough times we need to remember that things will get better, and we can look to past challenges to remind us just how resilient we really are. And while we are doing that, we can also own how we're feeling and let that be, too.

It's important to honor our uncomfortable feelings and let them be. If we feel like crying, cry. If we're scared, feeling hopeless or stuck, own and allow those feelings, too. What makes us unique and expressive people is we have feelings and sometimes our feelings are just plain uncomfortable. And then remember that feelings are like the tide; they come, and they go. They are part of the journey, but they are not the destination. You, my friend, are ultimately bound for glory. But for now, let those feelings in.

Live a Little

If you haven't been rejected, you haven't lived. We can dwell on the rejection, or we can seek out people who lift us up and then take a deep breath and shift our attention to moving forward with our days, our evenings and our lives.

Feeling rejected feels awful. It hurts. It impacts our self-esteem. We feel abandoned, lonely, angry, embarrassed, and unworthy. I am sure you could add other painful and sad feelings to the list. All of these feelings are legitimate and reasonable, but they also can distort reality. More often than not, being rejected isn't as personal as it certainly feels. And dwelling on these painful feelings doesn't help us feel better or move on.

So, feel what you feel and then take that deep breath. It's okay to shift your attention to other things, and then circle back to the sad feelings. Watch a funny movie or read a book. Go outside or make a gratitude list. Do something nice for someone. Then circle back and feel sad again. The point is not to deny your feelings; the intent is not to drown in them.

Now is Your Moment

Now is the time for calm and peaceful thoughts. Everything else can wait.

Just for today, take a break from all self-criticism. Remember that life is purposeful and evolving and you are growing and learning. Today, you have more inner resources than you did yesterday, and tomorrow, you will have even more. When you let yourself be, you create an opening for personal growth. It's that simple, that important, and that profound.

Ready and Willing

The deepest love always starts from within and radiates out. When we begin by loving ourselves just the way we are, our hearts and arms open to accept, embrace and love those around us just as they are, too.

When you are ready to own your uniqueness, your dreams and your potential, then you are finally ready to live the life that's been quietly waiting for you to step up and claim it. That's how we love ourselves. Are you ready, and are you willing? I know you are able.

A Reality Shift

A simple shift in perspective can change our moment, our day and our lives. Why not use this extraordinary power to shift your view of reality and see what happens to your attitude, your disposition, and your ability to move forward.

A shift in perspective isn't asking us to distort the truth but rather asks us to examine our current interpretation of the truth. When we decide to look at things from a different vantage point, we are just experimenting with the baggage and biases that we each bring to our view of our world. How we describe things to ourselves impacts how we feel, relate to others and move about our day. Asking yourself and your friends to consider another way of looking at things is a wild and wonderful experience.

We Still Have It

Sure, we're vulnerable and even needy, sometimes. But it's important to remember that even when we're feeling vulnerable, we still have the capacity to comfort and encourage others. Today, keep your eyes open for a 'helping' opportunity and create a day that makes someone else feel hopeful and you will discover that what you share is also what you receive.

We are all capable of being self-absorbed and self-focused. It's just part of being human and can be a good thing in moderation that actually helps get things done. But sometimes we need to give it a rest. If we are really the center of the universe, we need to imagine a bigger universe. One of the easiest and most effective ways to shift your focus is to begin paying attention to others. This can be family and friends, workmates, or even strangers. Spend some time and energy - and even resources - helping someone else. Not only is it important, the quality of your life and your universe will automatically expand. And when that happens for me, I am actually more content, happier and more grounded which are all good places to be to make things happen!

Channel Positive Energy

Whenever we share positive thoughts with others, we just naturally increase our capacity to receive positive energy in return. It's simple, powerful, and so easy to set in motion.

I have seen this in my own life. I think I first figured it out around negative emotions and expressions, like anger, jealousy, resentment. I then tried to flip it to a more positive practice. Try this for yourself and I think you'll discover that excitement, laughter, optimism, and kindness are all contagious, too. Why not start something good, even if you're feeling not so good? Maybe the good stuff will circle back and surprise you.

Powerful Thoughts

There is no need to minimize your pain, confusion or fear. But remember that your thoughts are powerful, and they either keep you in chains, or they set you free. We remain stuck when we accept powerlessness as fact, and we are set free by simply rejecting that concept and stepping out into the sunshine. With each small step towards the light, we are learning that we become more powerful by exercising the power we already have.

There are many days that could go in either direction. I have learned that there are things I can do that can impact or influence how my day goes. Playing showtunes on the radio rather than listening to the news is one example that works for me. I often choose the news and most often I may be informed or learn about the world's events, but at the same time it can fill me with stress or worry. Finding a balance and being informed are important to me. But too much of anything is too much.

Powerful Words

Words can be incredibly powerful, especially the words we use when talking to ourselves. Listen carefully. What are you telling yourself about your dreams, your goals, your hopes and the challenges you face? And as you listen, ask yourself if you need a re-write that is more positive, hopeful, and encouraging.

Sticks and stones may break our bones, but words can really hurt us, too. They can break our mood and spirit and sense of well-being. And although, we can't always control the words others share with us, we can control - with practice - the words we use when we're talking to ourselves. Here are some things we tell ourselves: "I am too old, too tall, too young, too short. I can't do math, or swim, or raise my hand and ask a question. I am stubborn, too easy, too fragile or too bossy." These are just a few examples, and if you pay attention, you'll begin to hear what you are telling yourself. You must be very careful about this because you're not only listening, but you're also believing.

Now, begin to rewrite your script. The easiest way to do it is to simply add the thought, "But I am going to try that anyway" or, "I am not going to let that get in the way." I've made a game of this in my own life, and a lot of things I used to tell myself were impossible, I am doing as we speak.

People Who Need People

It's essential to have people in our life to encourage and to remind us of our potential in a hopeful, optimistic and empowering way. We attract those people by being one of them.

As I have gotten older, I have become more discerning about who I want to spend time with, and more deliberate about who I invite into my life. It's clear that I want to spend my free time with authentic, emotionally available, hopeful people. I want to leave our time together feeling like we were good for each other. Often that includes laughter, honest and real conversations, and a natural curiosity about each other's lives. I like talking about my challenges, goals and hopes and my fears when our conversation is a two-way street. I need to both talk and listen.

Your Heart Knows

What your heart yearns for is not just a desire, it's a calling. It's up to you to listen and then follow. It's your pathway, plain and simple. And profoundly beautiful, too.

What does your heart yearn for? Trust your gut on this. Pretend you had 30 seconds to name it and then own it and see what happens next.

Work as a Blessing

If you are doing work you love and are passionate about, you are blessed beyond words. If you aren't there yet, but are taking steps to move in that direction, you are also blessed. And if you are just on the verge of discovering you deserve to be happy in your work, you are on the verge of being blessed.

I recently retired as the president and CEO of a large nonprofit organization that supports people with developmental and intellectual disabilities. The goal of all the services at this wonderful place is to create opportunities for others to have a good life and to help keep people living as independently as possible in their own communities. It was a job I loved, and even though I miss the people we served and the people I worked with, it was the right time to step down.

Retiring created space for me to move on in a bigger way to other things I wanted to do, including writing another book, preparing for an online class, and increasing my coaching availability. You can be sure I know how fortunate I've been with my career. But all that said, I can remember an earlier time in another job when I was very unhappy. I was underutilized, underappreciated and if I am honest, underperforming, too. I can remember how miserable and scared I was during that time, and I can remember how difficult it was to get to a better place. Getting there took many, many small steps, living through more than a couple great opportunities that didn't work out, and constantly asking myself, "Now, what?"

All this to say I know how it feels to be stuck and unhappy in a work situation and know how those small steps didn't always deliver quick results. But happy or not, I kept taking those steps and eventually ended up in a job that filled my heart, challenged my mind and convinced me that finding a way to safer ground doesn't always come easy or quickly but it waits for you.

A Perfect Circle

From the right vantage point, beginnings and endings are really all part of a much bigger circle. So, resist the temptation to fear either and trust that one day your beautiful circle will all make sense.

There is a Broadway song I have always loved. The lyrics invited us to open a new window or door and travel a highway we haven't traveled before. As that song reminds us, every day we have opportunities to open a new door or window and try something new. We can try big things like looking for a new job, leaving a relationship that isn't working or going back to school to learn a new skill that could lead to a new way to earn a living. And there are small ways, too, like listening to a different kind of music, or trying a type of food you've never tried, or even striking up conversations with people sitting beside you on the bus or subway.

Sometimes we plan endings and beginnings and sometimes they come unexpectedly out of left field. From the right vantage point, these beginnings and endings are all important parts of growth, life and your evolving journey.

The Million Dollar Answer

Life can be filled with so many distractions but remember this simple truth: you are here to love, and the most powerful and transforming love is manifested when you begin by loving yourself.

How do you love yourself? That is the million-dollar question, isn't it? I have learned that we are called to begin loving ourselves as we are, right now. Not when we finish the dishes or finish getting that degree. Not when we lose weight or stop making the same mistakes over and over. Not when we fix the things, we don't like about ourselves or change partners or jobs or save some money for retirement. The place to start is where you are. Be You. Love You. And then you can finish the dishes.

Pay It Forward

Instead of working at making life easier and better for ourselves, let's shift our focus to making it better and easier, for others.

One important thing I've discover for myself is I need to step away from all the confusion and noise and especially the news for just a bit. I need to get outside, somewhere where I can actually smell the ocean or touch a tree.

Here are a few things we can do: we can talk to our higher power as defined or as vague as that power may be, we can hug and comfort children, we can spend extra time with our pets, and we can be on the lookout for those who are all alone or lonely. As we share these little grounded in reality moments, we may catch a small but undeniable glimpse of light and hope that is very likely waiting for us around the next corner or two. I hope today you catch a glimpse and please know that I know how you feel because I feel it, too.

Lead by Example

It's not in your job description to make other people happy, but you can show them the way. You can light their path by following your passion, by living with integrity, empathy and kindness and by being present and helpful to those around you. But you can't make them happy. This is a simple and revolutionary idea that once grasped, is difficult to ignore.

All the time I've spent trying to fix people has not only been a complete waste of energy, but it's been time lost when I could have been taking care of business at home. Why do we act as if we need permission to focus on our own lives, our own course corrections, our own strengths we are trying to grow? I am not going to give you permission to focus on yourself because you don't need it. You are your own work of art, and it's unfolding, evolving, and beginning. You are a gift, and you've been given a piece of clay that you get to mold the way you want.

The world needs you to show up as you! Show people the way, offer to help when it's wanted, share the flower seeds you've been given but then get on with taking care of your own garden!

Into the World We Go

Today, let's focus less on what we want and more on what we have, less on our mistakes and more on our potential. And finally, let's do our best to spend less time in our heads and more time in our hearts. And with that, into the world we go.

We have the very real power of shifting our minds, our hearts and our spirit in incredibly beautiful ways. By being forgiving of ourselves and others, encouraging when we see our face in the mirror, and proud of how far we've come despite so many pitfalls or setbacks, we can begin to reshape how we think and feel in powerful ways. So today, and each day forward, lift your head high, take some deep breaths, and learn how to calm the chatter in your head. It will make space for beautiful things to come.

Closing

As we spend our final moments together, I'd like to share a few last-minute secrets you might find useful along the way, and one very short story that might help us end with a smile.

Let's begin with the secrets. I call them 'secrets' but they're really just things we need to remember. These fundamental truths were temporarily misplaced, and then most likely forgotten when you were still a child, but have been patiently waiting, just under the surface, to be rediscovered. Forgetting the lessons of childhood is the price we pay for growing older, but when we revisit some of them now, the timing can be perfect. Now they can be shaped into life-altering and life-affirming touchstones that will impact our lives in amazing and positive ways.

When secrets are buried, their power only grows stronger. With the scary secrets, we may need help unraveling how they have impacted our lives. With the more positive ones, we need to learn to welcome them with open arms. One last word about these reminders: don't worry if they seem a bit abstract or hard to wrap your arms around. Rather, simply react to them softly, and then just let them be. Once they are awakened, you don't really have to do anything else for them to be integrated into your life.

Secret Number One: Magic is everywhere.

This book is not an intellectual journey that will happen in your mind. The lessons that await you will be found somewhere in between the words and will only become transformative when understood by your heart. In other words, what you are about to experience is like a melody you can only hear when you stop thinking with your mind and begin listening with your heart. Now that you have been reminded that magic is everywhere, you will begin to notice it all around you, and it will enliven you even more.

Secret Number Two: When we allow ourselves to believe in magic, we become more intuitive.

Just sit with this for a moment. I know all the thoughts that swirl around in your mind can demand a great deal of your attention almost every second of every day. For now, try to give all of those distractions a rest. They will be waiting for you when you need it, but right now is not one of those times. Right now, we could all use a little more magic.

Secret Number Three: Trusting ourselves doesn't always come easy as adults, but it can be re-learned.

Trust is not always a feeling that comes as easily or as naturally as when we were children, and many of us are much more comfortable second-guessing, being skeptical or not listening to our hearts. Can you remember some of your missteps and mishaps that have happened because you couldn't, or rather didn't trust yourself? With a little practice, you will gradually get the hang of it, and the more you take a chance on trust, the easier trusting will become.

Secret Number Four: Your North Star is not a single star; it's a constellation.

We often yearn to know our one true purpose - our reason for being. But actually, we have so many purposes and they can change and fluctuate over time. It's funny that our quest to find our purpose is often viewed as difficult or challenging, or something that always seems to allude us. Many of us end up getting stuck and that contributes to the block we experience. For now, it's okay not to know your purpose. All you have to do is remain open.

Secret Number Five: Life is not always fair.

We don't really have the power to make life fairer for ourselves, but we have an extraordinary power to make life fairer for others. And when we use that power, the universe listens, our heart opens, and life is better. In other words, if you make life fairer for others, others will be making life fairer for you.

And it's worth noting that fairness isn't always about things. For example, if you mentor someone you work with so their job skills are enhanced, they get new skills and a chance for a better job. You, on the other hand, experience a sense of contributing and sharing something that you've been blessed with, and you get a sense of satisfaction. Gaining new skills makes things fairer for your co-worker and feeling content and grateful for your blessings makes things fairer for you.

Secret Number Six: Where you are right now is the perfect place to begin.

It's amazing what you can learn when you spend some quiet time alone with yourself. And it's astonishing and profoundly sad what you'll miss when you don't. Almost every answer you need is already deep within, and you owe it to yourself, your loved-ones, and the world to discover them without further delay. You are here, and therefore you are ready.

Secret Number Seven: You are perfectly imperfect.

If you are lonely or sad, this is for you. If you are anxious or frightened, or brokenhearted, this is for you, too. And if you are mourning the loss of a loved one or are feeling estranged from family or friends, this is also for you.

I am sorry that you are feeling this way right now and I want you to know that I have been there and I know how you feel. In fact, almost all people living lives and who are in touch with their feelings have been there and we all know these are very real, very hard and very human feelings to have.

I am not sure when or how you will move to calmer water but what I can tell you is that every storm passes eventually. If you can share with someone how you're feeling, please do that. If you need help, please reach out to others and let them help you. These words found you on purpose, you will get through this and there will be easier, better days ahead. I promise.

And one last short story before we part:

I recently saw the new Broadway musical *Hadestown* during previews (before the critics pronounced it a hit) and found it to be quite extraordinary. The night we saw it was actually the second night it was performed in New York, and before my partner Mike and I left the theatre, I had purchased an additional ticket to see it again. I was pretty sure this show was going to quickly become one of those impossible tickets to get and seeing it once would not be enough for me.

Because I'm a self-proclaimed 'theatre nerd,' I often strike up conversations with the people sitting next to me. I've learned that these conversations with strangers are a great way to meet new people, learn more about the play, and make new friends, too. This night was no exception. The man next to me was an older gentleman named Herbert, and during intermission I offered him a few pieces of my favorite candy – Junior Mints – and we began a wonderful conversation that actually made the night even more memorable for me.

Now, when I say, "older," given that I now am well passed the AARP membership age requirements myself, I would venture to guess that Herbert had at least 20 or 30 years on me. As we chatted, he quickly solved that mystery by telling me he had just turned 98-years-old! Lately I have found myself searching for and quietly celebrating people older than me who are still living exciting and engaged lives, just like Herbert. I popped another Junior Mint into my mouth and grinned.

I had noticed Herbert watching me during the first act of the play and had a feeling it might have been because the man I was with had his arm around me while we watched the musical. I had thought, because of his age, that maybe Herbert was uncomfortable or even judging me.

I was wrong.

Instead, Herbert told me he was having fun watching me move to the music and said he noticed my leg bouncing and foot tapping along with the score. I then thought this was his way of kindly telling me to 'tone it down' a bit, but he laughed and said he was simply enjoying me, enjoying the show. He went on to say that he had seen an earlier version of the show a while back off-Broadway and loved it then, too. As we talked about the amazing set, the group of talented actors and the beautiful toe-tapping music, he mentioned that the director of *Hadestown* was actually his great granddaughter, Rachel Chavkin.

I knew of Rachel because I had been reading about this talented, up-and-coming, innovative, young theater director and knew that Herbert had a very good reason to be beaming with pride. And now I was beaming, too, because our conversation had added a wonderful new layer of wonder to our budding friendship.

When the lights dimmed, Herbert and I stopped chatting and I put the candy back in my pocket. And then faster than I would have wished, the last song was sung and the entire audience was quickly on their feet with enthusiastic applause. As I took a second to stand up, I offered Herbert my arm to help him as well, and together we joined hundreds of people joyfully expressing their enthusiastic gratitude for what we had all just shared.

The 98-year-old man beside me probably didn't realize it, but as we sat side-by-side that night, he had touched and inspired me in a profound way.

Helping Herbert to his feet was a powerful moment for me because as we stood, I quietly acknowledged my hope that theatre would always be a part of my life. And also, because in that moment I trusted that as I grow closer to my own personal 'curtain call,' that one night, somewhere in a darkened theatre somewhere, the universe would sit me beside someone who would quietly offer an arm to help me to my feet, too.

And there you have it.

When you and I began this book together, we started a journey. And if you've spent a little time within its pages, I think you'd agree that, especially now, we do know each other. That makes me happy.

See you around!

Love, Paul

Acknowledgements

If I truly mentioned everyone who deserved a thank-you, this book would never be finished. There are so many important people who I appreciate and love, and who have helped me turn all kinds of dreams into realities. I am very fortunate to be able to count on them to be there when I have needed courage, comfort and hope.

If you are part of my immediate biological family, you already know how much I love and adore you with all my heart. Simply spending any amount of time laughing, or just celebrating the true love we all share, is the greatest gift I have ever been given.

If you are part of my chosen family, you know who you are, so I hope you smile when you read this. I love you dearly, and feel like we are destined to be together, evermore.

To my friends in our *Begin with Yes* online community, you are the sole reason I keep writing books. I have learned so much from you and I love to visit with you, each and every day. We encourage, learn and support each other there, and it's a powerful place where good things happen.

I want to especially thank Teresa Dainesi, my talented, always-giving confidant, trusted friend, and editor of this book. We collectively worked on this manuscript during some individual stormy weather, and trust me when I say we both know, first-hand, how important courage, comfort and hope really are.

And, finally, to our amazing goldendoodle, Toby. While it may seem unusual to dedicate this to a dog, the lessons he has taught us have been immeasurable. We always look to him as a role model and a benchmark of real love. If the world could be half as loving as Toby is to us, it would be a very different place. Mike and I feel so lucky and blessed he has graced our lives.

I am grateful to each and every one of you who has accompanied me on this beautiful journey.

Paul is also lucky to work with Dave Bastien, a mastermind behind everything technical, creative, and beyond, and Jamie Barone, a true social media guru who makes sure his content is up every day. Because of these two amazing pros, he has time to write and be engaged with folks on his social media pages, including: *Begin with Yes* and *Be Amazing.*

You can find Paul at beginwithyes.com and join his Facebook community at facebook.com/beginwithyes. You can also write to Paul about keynotes, personal coaching, or just to say hello at: paul@beginwithyes.com.

Biography

Paul Boynton is an international bestselling author, motivational speaker, a popular social media influencer, and a believer in dreams, goals and making things happen.

As a trained social worker and therapist, his career spanned over 50 years in the healthcare, human services, and nonprofit sectors, most recently as CEO of an award-winning nonprofit helping individuals with developmental and intellectual disabilities become more productive, fulfilled members of their community.

His first book, *Begin with Yes*, was recently released in a 10th Anniversary Edition with a foreword by actress Jane Seymour. His second manuscript, *Be Amazing*, was distributed by Simon and Schuster. His writing is often featured in *HuffPost*, and his online social media presence has amassed well over two million followers who credit him as a source of inspiration for taking steps toward a more meaningful, purpose-driven life.

PAUL S. BOYNTON

163

PAUL S. BOYNTON